# MIRROR OF WISDOM

D0188415

Geshe Tsultim Gyeltsen

# MIRROR OF WISDOM
## *Teachings on Emptiness*

Commentaries on
the emptiness section of *Mind Training Like the Rays of the Sun*
and *The Heart Sutra*

Translated by Lotsawa Tenzin Dorjee

Edited by Rebecca McClen Novick, Linda Gatter
and Nicholas Ribush

Produced by the LAMA YESHE WISDOM ARCHIVE, Boston, Massachusetts
for
Thubten Dhargye Ling Publications, Long Beach, California
www.tdling.com

First published 2000
10,000 copies for free distribution


Thubten Dhargye Ling
PO Box 90665
Long Beach
CA 90809, USA

ISBN 0-9623421-5-7


10 9 8 7 6 5 4 3 2 1


Front cover: Manjushri, the Buddha of Wisdom, painted
by Ala Rigta
Back cover photo by Don Farber
Designed by Mark Gatter

Printed in Canada

Published on the auspicious occasion of His Holiness the
Dalai Lama's visit to Los Angeles, June, 2000, sponsored
by Thubten Dhargye Ling

# CONTENTS

# PUBLISHER'S NOTE

Buddha Shakyamuni taught the *Perfection of Wisdom,* otherwise known as the *Wisdom Gone Beyond,* on Vulture's Peak, Rajgir, in what is today the Indian state of Bihar.

These sutras focus on the subject of emptiness, the ultimate nature of reality, and the *Heart Sutra* is one of the most significant. It is a beautifully condensed version of the Buddha's teachings on emptiness, containing their essential meaning in only a few lines. Geshe Gyeltsen tells us that by integrating this teaching with our minds, it is possible for us to become enlightened within a single lifetime.

*Mind Training Like the Rays of the Sun* was authored by Namkha Pel, a close student of the great Tibetan scholar and yogi, Lama Tsong Khapa. It is a commentary to the *Seven Point Mind Training,* which was composed by the Kadampa master, Geshe Chekawa. The mind training tradition was introduced to Tibet by the renowned Indian master Atisha and contains practices for generating bodhicitta, the altruistic attitude that seeks enlightenment for the sake of others. In this book, Geshe Gyeltsen focuses on the emptiness section of Namkha Pel's text.

The subject of emptiness is very profound. Here, Geshe-la gives us clear and extensive instructions on the topic so that we may come to understand and experience its meaning. The realization of the wisdom of emptiness is vital to our spiritual development. As Geshe-la says, "We must realize that all the suffering we experience comes from the delusions in our mind. In order to cut through these delusions, we need the weapon of the wisdom perceiving emptiness."

Geshe Gyeltsen gave this commentary on the *Heart Sutra* over a period of months, beginning in May, 1994, when his center, Thubten Dhargye Ling, was still located in West Los Angeles. By the time he gave the teachings on the emptiness section of *Mind Training Like the Rays of the Sun* in September, 1996, Thubten Dhargye Ling had moved to its present location in Long Beach.

Thubten Dhargye Ling Publications extend our deepest gratitude to Geshe-la for giving these teachings, to Lotsawa Tenzin Dorjee for translating them into English and to Hung The Quach for interpreting for the Vietnamese students. We are also grateful to Rebecca McClen Novick, Linda Gatter and Nicholas Ribush for editing this work for publication, to Mark Gatter for designing the book and to the LAMA YESHE WISDOM ARCHIVE for supervising its production. Many thanks are also due to Venerable Ani Tenzin Kachö, who assisted in the transcribing of *Mind Training Like the Rays of the Sun*; to Linh Phuy, the translator of the Vietnamese edition of this book; to Doren Harper for initiating and organizing this project; and to Doren and Mary Harper for offering most of the funds required for publication.

We extend heartfelt thanks as well to the following generous contributors: Iku Bacon, Angie Barkmeijer de Wit, Karen Bennike, Jeff Bickford, Roger Bosse, Bill & Margie Brown, Christina Cao, Regina Dipadova, Annie Do, Walter Drake, Michael Fogg, Jim & Sesame Fowler, Robert Friedman, Matthew Frum, Eric W. Gruenwald, Gail Gustafson, Bev Gwyn, Alisha & Rachelle Harper, Robin Hart, Elwood & Linda Higgley, Thao X. Ho, Elaine Jackson, John Jackson, Leslie A. Jamison, Ven. Tenzin Kachö, Paul, Trisha, Rachel & Daniel Kane, Judy Kann, Donald Kardok, Barbara Lee, Oanh N. Mai, Vicky Manchester, Maryanne Miss, Michael & Bonnie Moore, Terrence Moore, Tam Nguyen, Quan K. Pham, Thanh Mai Pham, Richard Prinz, Gary Renlau, Gary & Sandy Schlageter, David & Susan Schwartz, Stuart & Lillie Scudder, Charlotte Tang, Christel Taylor and Shasta & Angelica Wallace.

We are also deeply grateful to the many benefactors who asked to remain anonymous and to those kind people whose donations were made after this book went to press. We'll mention you next time! Thank you all so much.

Last but not least, we offer sincere thanks in general to all the students of Thubten Dhargye Ling and our other centers for their devotion to and constant support of our kind teacher, Geshe Tsultim Gyeltsen, and his far-reaching Dharma work.

# Part One

# A Commentary on the Emptiness Section of
## of
## *Mind Training Like the Rays of the Sun*

# ONE

# INTRODUCTION

## MOTIVATION

Please take a moment to cultivate the altruistic motivation of seeking complete enlightenment for the sake of liberating all sentient beings throughout space. It is with this kind of motivation, which we call the motivation of bodhicitta, that you should participate in this teaching. It is very important that you don't read or listen to teachings simply because someone else coerces or expects you to do so. Your involvement should spring from your own wish to practice the teachings with the aim of accomplishing enlightenment for yourself as well as for others. As you apply yourself to this mind training practice, you should do so full of sincerity and whole-heartedness. If you have a wavering or doubting mind, it will negatively affect your practice.

In the *lam-rim*—the treatises on the graduated path to enlightenment—the great Tibetan master Lama Tsong Khapa states that if our mind is positive and wholesome we will attain positive and wholesome results. Cultivating a good attitude motivates us to engage in positive actions and these return positive results to us. If our attitude and motivation are negative, however, we will create negative actions that will bring us unwanted pains and problems. Everything depends on the mind.

This is why the teacher or lama always advises the audience to cultivate a proper motivation at the beginning of every teaching. The historical Buddha often advised his disciples that they should listen well, listen thoroughly and hold the teachings in their minds. At the beginning of the lam-rim, there is an outline that states that the audience should be free from what are known as "the three faults of the container." When Buddha said, "Listen well," he meant that when we participate in the teachings we should do so with pure motivation. We should be like an uncontaminated vessel—a clean pot. When he said, "Listen thoroughly," he meant that the listener should not be like a container or pot that is turned upside-down because nothing will be able to enter it. And when Buddha said, "Hold the teachings in your mind," he meant that the listener should not be like a leaky pot, one that does not retain its contents; in other words, we should try to remember the teachings that are given.

The simple reason we all need spirituality, especially Dharma, in our lives is because it is the source of true peace and happiness for ourselves as well as for others. It is the perfect solution for the unwanted problems and pains we face in this cycle of existence, or samsara. For example, we all know that if there were no food or drink in the world, then our very existence would be threatened because these are the basic necessities of life. Food and drink are related to the sustenance of this earthly life, but Dharma is much more important because it is through Dharma that we can remove the misconceptions and ignorance, which cause all our deeper problems. The Tibetan word for Dharma is *nang-chö*, which means "inner science" or "inner knowledge." This tells us that all of the Buddha's teaching is primarily aimed at subduing the inner phenomenon of our mind.

In this way, we begin to understand the significance and necessity of Dharma in our lives. As we learn to appreciate the Dharma more and more it enables us to do a better job of coping with the difficulties we encounter. With this understanding and appreciation we will then feel enthusiastic about applying ourselves to spirituality. We will find ourselves cherishing the Dharma as if it were a precious treasure from which we wish to never part. For example, if we possess some gold we are naturally going to cherish it. We're not going to dump it in the trash because we know its value and what it can do for us. Yet the value of gold is limited to only this existence; when we die we can't take even a speck of gold with us. But spirituality is something that follows us into our future lives. If we don't practice Dharma then our spiritual life, which exists forever, will be threatened.

Having become an enlightened being, Buddha showed us the complete path leading to liberation and enlightenment. He did this out of his total love and compassion, without any kind of selfish motive. The kind of love we are talking about is the wish that everyone will have true peace and happiness and the best of everything. Compassion means the wish that everyone will be free from all kinds of suffering. The best way to follow the Buddha's teachings is to do our own practice with this kind of attitude and motivation.

It may seem that this world is filled with people who generally don't appear to care about spirituality at all. So why should *we* care so much? But the fact that these people don't care for spirituality doesn't mean that they don't need it. Every sentient being needs spirituality, from humans down to the smallest insect living beneath the earth. The wish for lasting peace and happiness and the wish to be free from any kind of suffering is not something exclusive to us; it is something that is shared by all sentient beings. However, many people don't realize the value of spirituality and do not have access to the Dharma. In his *Ornament for Clear Realizations*, Maitreya states, "Even if the king of divine beings brings down a rain upon the earth, unsuitable seeds will never germinate. In the same way, when enlightened beings come to the world, those who do not have the fortune to meet them can never taste the nectar of Dharma."

So, we shouldn't look down on those who don't engage in spirituality or consider them to be bad people; it is just that they have not been fortunate enough to encounter spirituality and put it into practice. This is a good reason to extend our compassion to them. Like us, they seek true peace and happiness, but unlike us, they do not have the means to find what they desire. Basically, there is no difference between us and them—we are all in the same boat—but at the same time, we should appreciate our own great fortune in having the opportunity to participate in the Dharma. Understanding this, we should develop the strong determination that in this lifetime we will do our best to study and practice spirituality in order to take the best care of our future lives. We should try to remind ourselves of these points as often as possible.

It is important for us to understand that all our Dharma actions are very valuable, whether we are studying or listening to spiritual teachings, giving spiritual teaching to others or engaging in our practice. Whatever Dharma teaching we practice we must be sure that it is helping us to transform our state of mind for the better. We have to integrate the Dharma with our own mental state. If, as we study, we leave a gap between our mind and the Dharma, we defeat the purpose of spiritual practice. We wear the Dharma like an ornament and, like an ornament, it might look attractive, but it does not affect us on the inside.

If we want to grow a tree, we need to water the soil around the seed. It's not enough just to fill a bucket with water and leave it near the field. This is sometimes the case with our practice. Burying ourselves in all kinds of Dharma books and other publications and collecting intellectual knowledge about the Dharma is not sufficient. What is required is that we apply the Dharma to our own lives so that we bring about positive changes in the actions of our body, speech and mind. Then we get the true benefit of the Dharma and manifest such changes as can be seen by other people.

Let's examine where our unwanted pains and problems come from. For example, most of you work all day and keep yourselves busy mentally and physically. You would probably rather relax, so what is it that makes you rush about leading such a busy life? What is it that makes you work like a slave, beyond trying to pay the rent or feed your family? Maybe you get upset over some disagreement or maybe your mind becomes disturbed and as a result you also become physically tense. Or perhaps, due to some kind of sickness, both your mind and body become unsettled. You have to find the root cause of all such problems and difficulties of daily life.

The fact of the matter is, eventually all of us must die. After we die, we have to take rebirth. We need to discover what precipitates our rebirth in "bad migrations"—the negative situations of the hell, hungry ghost and animal realms. Even when we take a very good rebirth, we still experience many problems related to work, health, aging, dying and death. We have to determine the underlying cause of all these difficulties.

First, what is it that experiences all these problems? Is it only beings with a mind or do even inanimate objects experience them? Secondly, what creates these problems—mind or inanimate phenomena? The answer to both questions is the mind. Only mind can experience and create all the kinds of suffering that we and others go through. Is it another's mind that creates our problems and puts us through all this hell or is it our own mind that creates them? The minds of others cannot create the difficulties that we as individual people go through, just as the karmic actions of others cannot cause our problems. You cannot experience the karma created by others. That is simply not part of the law of karmic action and result. You don't have to take this on faith; it is a good idea to investigate this matter from your own side.

If we continue to study and practice, one of these days we will be able to see the kind of problematic situations we create for ourselves. We will see that motivated by delusion, we engage in all kinds of wrong karmic actions, which cause us pain and difficulty.

Now I am going to comment on a text called *Mind Training Like the Rays of the Sun*, which is Namkha Pel's commentary on the *Seven Point Mind Training* text composed by the great master, Geshe Chekawa. It belongs to a special category of Buddhist texts called *lojong*, which means "mind training" or "thought transformation." The mind training system provides methods to train and transform our minds and focuses on how to generate great love (*mahamaitri*), great compassion (*mahakaruna*) and the altruistic mind of enlightenment (*bodhicitta*).

When we read different Buddhist treatises or listen to different teachings on the same topic, we should try to bring together our understanding from many different sources. When we work on a project we use both hands. Our left and right hands don't clash but rather complement each other and work in unison. In the same way, we should bring whatever understanding we gain from studying different texts concerning a specific topic, to augment and complement our practice.

WHAT IS A BUDDHIST?

The Tibetan word for Buddhist is *nang-pa,* which literally means "one who is focused on inner reality." This refers to someone who concentrates more on his or her inner world than on external phenomena. This is perhaps the most important point regarding Buddhist practice. Our primary goal is to subdue and transform our state of mind—our inner reality. In this way, we seek to improve all our actions of body and speech, but especially those of mind.

I occasionally observe that some people modify their external actions while internally there isn't any kind of positive change going on at all. Things might even be deteriorating. Even as we try to practice the Buddhist teachings, our delusions of ignorance, attachment, anger and so forth become more rampant. When this happens, it is not because there is something wrong with our spiritual path. It is because our own faulty actions contaminate the teachings and therefore we cannot experience the complete results of our practice. When such things happen, it is very important not to let go of our practice. Instead, we should understand that in some way we are not properly applying the teachings to ourselves.

How do we distinguish Buddhists from non-Buddhists? A Buddhist is someone who has gone for refuge from the depths of his or her heart to what are known as the Three Jewels or the Triple Gem—the Jewel of Buddha, the Jewel of Dharma and the Jewel of Sangha. Having gone for refuge to the Jewel of Buddha, we should be careful not to follow misleading guides or teachers. Having taken refuge in the Jewel of Dharma, we should not harm any sentient being no matter what its size. Furthermore, we should cultivate compassion, the wish to ensure that all beings are free from unwanted mental and physical problems. And having taken refuge in the Jewel of the Sangha, or the spiritual community, we should not participate in a club, group or organization that brings harm to ourselves or other beings.

We need to try to discover the source of our own and others' suffering and then find out what path or method we can use to destroy it. The next thing is to apply ourselves enthusiastically and consistently to this method. If we do that, we will be able to free ourselves from all kinds of suffering, which means that we will free ourselves from samsara, help others free themselves from samsara and eventually attain the state of highest enlightenment.

## WHAT IS BUDDHA NATURE?

Buddha nature is the latent potentiality for becoming a buddha, or enlightened being—it is the seed of enlightenment. There are two kinds of buddha nature—"naturally abiding buddha nature" and "developable buddha nature." According to Theravada Buddhism, there are certain beings that do not have buddha nature, but from the Mahayana perspective, every sentient being down to the smallest insect has both seeds of enlightenment within them. Even a person who is incredibly evil and negative still has these two buddha natures, both of which can be activated sometime in the future.

This does not mean that people who are making a great effort to accomplish enlightenment and those who do no spiritual practice at all are no different from each other. For those who don't practice, realization of their buddha nature is only a mere possibility and it will take them an unimaginably long time to become enlightened. Others, who are striving for enlightenment, will reach that state much faster because what they are practicing is actually contributing towards the activation their buddha nature.

There are three levels of bodhi, or enlightenment. There is the enlightenment of hearers, or *shravakas*; the enlightenment of solitary realizers, or *pratyekabuddhas*; and the enlightenment of the Greater Vehicle, or Mahayana. It is the latter that we are discussing here—the highest form of enlightenment, the enlightenment of bodhisattvas. It is a unique characteristic of Mahayana Buddhism that each of us who follows and cultivates the path as a practitioner can eventually become a buddha, or enlightened person. We may doubt our ability to become an enlightened being, but the truth is that we all share the same potential.

Developable buddha nature and naturally abiding buddha nature are posited from the point of view of potencies that can eventually transform into enlightened bodies. Our naturally abiding buddha nature eventually enables us to achieve the truth body of enlightenment, the state of dharmakaya. The form body of enlightenment, or rupakaya, is called "developable" buddha nature because it can be developed, eventually transforming into rupakaya. If all the favorable conditions are created then these buddha natures, or seeds, will germinate on the spiritual path and bloom into the fruit of enlightenment. However, if we just keep on waiting around thinking, "Well, eventually I am going to become a buddha anyway, so I don't have to do anything," we will never get anywhere. The seeds of enlightenment must be activated through our own effort.

## COMPASSION AND BODHICITTA

Bodhicitta is the altruistic mind of enlightenment. There is conventional bodhicitta, or the conventional mind of enlightenment, and there is ultimate bodhicitta, or the ultimate mind of enlightenment. Bodhicitta is the bodhisattva's "other-oriented" attitude—it is the gateway to Mahayana Buddhism. The wisdom perceiving emptiness is not the entrance to Mahayana Buddhism because it is common to both Theravada and Mahayana. Hearers and solitary realizers also cultivate the wisdom of emptiness in order to realize their spiritual goals.

Before we can actually experience bodhicitta we must experience great compassion. The Sanskrit word for great compassion is *mahakaruna*. The word *karuna* means "stopping happiness." This might sound like a negative goal but it is not. When you cultivate great compassion, it stops you from seeking the happiness of nirvana for yourself alone. As Maitreya puts it in his *Ornament for Clear Realizations*, "With compassion, you don't abide in the extreme of peace." What this means is that with great compassion you don't seek only personal liberation, or nirvana. Compassion is the root of the Buddha's teaching, especially the Mahayana. Whenever anyone develops and experiences great compassion, he or she is said to have the Mahayana spiritual inclination and to have become a member of the Mahayana family. We may not have such compassion at the present time; nonetheless, we should be aspiring to achieve it.

# Two

# MIND TRAINING, DEVELOPING BODHICITTA

## PRELIMINARIES

We should always begin our study and practice at the basic level and slowly ascend the ladder of practice. First of all, we should learn about going for refuge in the Three Jewels of Buddha, Dharma and Sangha and put that into practice. Then we should study and follow the law of karmic actions and their results. Next, we should meditate on the preciousness of our human life, our great spiritual potential and upon our own death and the impermanence of our body. After that we should develop an awareness of our own state of mind and notice what it is really doing. If we are thinking of harming anyone, even the smallest insect, then we must let go of that thought, but if our mind is thinking of something positive, such as wishing to help and cherish others, then we must try to enhance that quality. As we progress, we slowly train our mind in bodhicitta and go on to study the perfect view of emptiness. This is the proper way to approach Buddhist study and practice.

As we engage in our practice of Dharma there will be definite signs of improvement. Of course, these signs should come from within. The great Kadampa master, Geshe Chekawa, states, "Change or transform your attitude and leave your external conduct as it is." What he is telling us is that we should direct our attention towards bringing about positive transformation within, but in terms of our external conduct we should still behave without pretense, like a normal person. We should not be showy about any realization we have gained or think that we have license to conduct ourselves in any way we like. As we look into our own mind, if we find that delusions such as anger, attachment, arrogance and jealousy are diminishing and feel more intent on helping others, that is a sign that positive change is taking place.

Lama Tsong Khapa stated that in order to get rid of our confusion with regard to any subject, we must develop the three wisdoms that arise through contemplation. We have to listen to the relevant teaching, which develops the "wisdom through hearing." Then we contemplate the meaning of the teaching, which gives rise to the "wisdom of contemplation." Finally, we meditate on the ascertained meaning of the teaching, which gives rise to the "wisdom of meditation." By applying these three kinds of wisdom, we will be able to get beyond our doubts, misconceptions and confusion.

INVESTIGATING OUR ACTIONS

The text advises that we should apply ourselves to gross analysis (conceptual investigation) and subtle analysis (analytical investigation) to find out if we are performing proper actions with our body, speech and mind. If we are, then there is nothing more to do. However, if we find that certain actions of our body, speech and mind are improper, we should correct ourselves.

Every action that we perform has a motivation at its beginning. We have to investigate and analyze whether this motivation is positive or negative. If we discover that we have a negative motivation, we have to let go of that and adopt a positive one. Then, while we're actually performing the action, we have to investigate whether our action is correct or not. Finally, once we have completed the action, we have to end it with a dedication and again, analyze the correctness of our dedication. In this way, we observe the three phases of our every action of body, speech and mind, letting go of the incorrect actions and adopting the correct ones.

We should do this as often as we can, but we should try to do it at least three times a day. First thing in the morning, when we get up from our beds, we should analyze our mind and set up the right motivation for the day. During the day we should again apply this mindfulness to our actions and activities. Then in the evening, before we go to bed, we should review our actions of the daytime.

If we find that we did something that we shouldn't have, we should regret the wrong action and develop contrition for having engaged in it and determine not to engage in that action again. It is essential that we purify our negativities, or wrong actions, in this way. However, if we find that we have committed good actions, we should feel happy. We should appreciate our own positive actions and draw inspiration from them, determining that tomorrow we should try to do the same or even better.

Buddha said, "Taking your own body as an example, do not harm others." So, taking ourselves as an example, what do we want? We want real peace, happiness and the best of everything. What do we not want? We don't want any kind of pain, problem or difficulty. Everyone else has the same wish—so, with that kind of understanding we should stop harming others, including those who we see as our enemies. His Holiness the Dalai Lama often advises that if we can't help others, then we should at least not harm them, either through our speech or our physical actions. In fact, we shouldn't even *think* harmful thoughts.

PRACTICING PATIENCE

The text states that we should not be boastful. Instead, we should appreciate the good actions we've performed. If you go up to people and say, "Haven't I been kind to you?" nobody will appreciate what you've done. In the *Eight Verses of Mind Training*, we read that even if people turn out to be ungrateful to us and say or do nasty things when we have been kind and helpful to them, we should make all the more effort to appreciate the great opportunity they have provided us to develop our patience. The stanza ends beautifully, "Bless me to be able to see them as if they were my true teachers of patience." After all, they are providing us with a real chance to practice patience, not just a hypothetical one. That is exactly what mind training is. When we find ourselves in that kind of difficult situation, we should just stay cool and realize that we have a great opportunity to practice *kshantiparamita,* the "perfection of patience."

In the same vein, the text also advises us not to be short-tempered. We shouldn't let ourselves be shaken by difficult circumstances or situations. Generally, when people say nice things to us or bring us gifts, we feel happy. On the other hand, if someone says the smallest thing that we don't want to hear, we get upset. Don't be like that. We need to remain firm in our practice and maintain our peace of mind.

## DEVELOPING CONSISTENCY

The text reminds us to practice our mind training with consistency. We shouldn't practice for a few days and then give it up because we've decided it's not working. At first, we may apply ourselves very diligently to study and practice out of a sense of novelty or because we've heard so much about the benefits of meditation. Then, in a day or two, we stop because we don't think we're making any progress. Or, for a while we may come to the teachings before everyone else but then we just give up and disappear, making all kinds of reasons and excuses for our behavior. That won't help.

If we keep in mind that our ultimate goal is to become completely enlightened, then we can begin to comprehend the length of time we'll need for practice. The great Indian master, Chandrakirti, says that all kinds of accomplishments follow from diligence, consistency and enthusiasm. If we apply ourselves correctly to the proper practice we will eventually reach our destination. He says that if we don't have constant enthusiasm, even if we are very intelligent we are not going to achieve very much. Intelligence is like a drawing made on water but constant enthusiasm in our practice is like a carving made in rock—it remains for a much longer time.

So, whatever practice each of us does, big or small, if we do it consistently, over the course of time we will find great progress within ourselves. One of the examples used in Buddhist literature is that our enthusiasm should be constant, like the flow of a river. Another example compares consistency to a strong bowstring. If a bowstring is straight and strong, we can shoot the arrow further. We read in a text called *The Praise of the Praiseworthy,* "For you to prove your superiority, show neither flexibility nor rigidity." The point being made here is that we should be moderate in applying ourselves to our practice. We should not rigidly overexert ourselves for a short duration and then stop completely, but neither should we be too flexible and relaxed, because then we become too lethargic.

## EXPECTATIONS OF REWARD

The next advice given in the text is that we should not anticipate some reward as soon as we do something nice. When we practice giving, or generosity, the best way to give is selflessly and unconditionally. That is great giving. In Buddhist scriptures we find it stated that as a result of our own giving and generosity, we acquire the possessions and resources we need. When we give without expecting anything in return, our giving will certainly bring its result, but when we give with the gaining of resources as our motivation, our giving becomes somewhat impure. Intellectualizing, thinking, "I must give because giving will bring something back to me," contaminates our practice of generosity.

When we give we should do so out of compassion and understanding. We have compassion for the poor and needy, for example, because we can clearly see their need. Sometimes people stop giving to the homeless because they think that they might go to a bar and get drunk or otherwise use the gift unwisely. We should remember that when we give to others, we never have any control over how the recipient uses our gift. Once we have given something, it has become the property of the other person. It's up to them to decide what they will do with it.

## KARMIC ACTIONS

Another cardinal point of Buddhism concerns karmic actions. Sometimes we go through good times in our lives and sometimes we go through bad; but we should understand that all these situations are related to our own personal karmic actions of body, speech and mind. Shakyamuni Buddha taught numerous things intended to benefit three kinds of disciples—those who are inclined to the Hearers' Vehicle, those who are inclined to the Solitary Realizers' Vehicle and those who are inclined to the Greater Vehicle. Buddha said to all three kinds of prospective disciples, "You are your own protector." In other words, if you want to be free from any kind of suffering, it is your own responsibility to find the way and to follow it. Others cannot do it for you. No one can present the way to liberation as if it were a gift. You are totally responsible for yourself.

"You are your own protector." That statement is very profound and carries a deep message for us. It also implicitly speaks about the law of karmic actions and results. You are responsible for your karmic actions—if you do good, you will have good; if you do bad, you will have bad. It's as simple as that. If you don't create and accumulate a karmic action, you will never meet its results. Also, the karmic actions that you have already created and accumulated are not simply going to disappear. It is just a matter of time and the coming together of certain conditions for these karmic actions to bring forth their results.

When we directly, or non-conceptually, fully realize emptiness, from that moment on we will never create any new karmic seeds to be reborn in cyclic existence. It is true that transcendent bodhisattvas return to samsara, but they don't come back under the influence of contaminated karmic actions or delusions. They return out of their will power, their aspirational prayers and their great compassion.

THE DESIRE TO BE LIBERATED

Without the sincere desire to be free from cyclic existence, it is impossible to become liberated from it. In order to practice with enthusiasm, we must cultivate the determined wish to be liberated from the miseries of cyclic existence. We can develop this enthusiastic wish by contemplating the suffering nature of samsara, this cycle of compulsive rebirths in which we find ourselves. As Lama Tsong Khapa states in his beautifully concise text, the *Three Principal Paths*, without the pure, determined wish to be liberated, one will not be able to let go of the prosperity and goodness of cyclic existence. What he is saying—and our own experience will confirm this—is that we tend to focus mostly, and perhaps most sincerely, on the temporary pleasures and happiness of this lifetime. As we do this, we get more and more entrenched in cyclic existence.

In order to break this bond to samsara, it is imperative that we cultivate the determined wish for liberation, and to do that we have to follow certain steps. First, we must try to sever our attachment and clinging to the temporary marvels and prosperity of this lifetime. Then we need to do the same thing with regard to our future lives. No matter whether we are seeking personal liberation or complete enlightenment for the benefit of all sentient beings, we must first cultivate this attitude of renunciation. Having done that, if we want to find our own personal liberation, or nirvana, then we can follow the path of hearers or solitary realizers, but if we want to work for the betterment of all sentient beings, we should at that point follow Greater Vehicle Buddhism—the path of the bodhisattvas—which leads to the highest state of enlightenment.

The determined wish to be liberated is the first path of Lama Tsong Khapa's *Three Principal Paths*, which presents the complete path to enlightenment. Tsong Khapa said that this human life, with its freedoms and enriching factors, is more precious than a wish-fulfilling gem. He also tells us that, however valuable and filled with potential our life is, it is as transient as lightning. We must understand that worldly activities are as frivolous and meaningless as husks of grain. Discarding them, we should engage instead in spiritual practice to derive the essence of this wonderful human existence.

We need to realize the preciousness and rarity of this human life and our great spiritual potential as well as our life's temporary nature and the impermanence of all things. However, we should not interpret this teaching as meaning that we should devalue ourselves. It simply means that we should release our attachment and clinging to this life because they are the main source of our problems and difficulties. We also need to release our attachment and clinging to our future lives and their particular marvels and pleasures. As a way of dealing with this attachment, we need to contemplate and develop conviction in the infallibility of the law of karmic actions and their results and then contemplate the suffering nature of cyclic existence.

How do we know when we have developed the determined wish to be liberated? Lama Tsong Khapa says that if we do not aspire to the pleasures of cyclic existence for even a moment but instead, day in and day out, find ourselves naturally seeking liberation, then we can say that we have developed the determined wish to be liberated. If we were to fall into a blazing fire pit, we wouldn't find even one moment that we wanted to be there. There'd be nothing enjoyable about it at all and we would want to get out immediately. If we develop that kind of determination regarding cyclic existence, then that is a profound realization. Without even the aspiration to develop renunciation, we will never begin to seek enlightenment and therefore will not engage in the practices that lead us towards it.

MOTIVATION FOR SEEKING ENLIGHTENMENT

There are three kinds of motivation we can have for aspiring to attain freedom from the sufferings of cyclic existence. The lowest motivation seeks a favorable rebirth in our next life, such as the one we have right now. With this motivation we will be able to derive the smallest essence from our human life.

The intermediate level of motivation desires complete liberation from samsara and is generating by reflecting upon the suffering nature of cyclic existence and becoming frightened of all its pains and problems. The method that can help us attain this state of liberation is the study of the common paths of the *Tripitaka*, the Three Baskets of teachings, and the practice and cultivation of the common paths of the three higher trainings—ethics, concentration and wisdom. This involves meditating on emptiness and developing the wisdom that realizes emptiness as the ultimate nature of all phenomena. As a result of these practices, we are then able to counteract and get rid of all 84,000 delusions and reach the state of liberation. With this intermediate motivation we achieve the state of lasting peace and happiness for ourselves alone. Our spiritual destination is personal nirvana.

The highest level of motivation is the altruistic motivation of bodhicitta—seeking complete enlightenment for the sake of all sentient beings. With this kind of motivation, we are affirming the connections we have made with all sentient beings over many lifetimes. All sentient beings are recognized as having once been our mothers, fathers and closest friends. We appreciate how kind they have been to us and we develop the responsibility of helping them to become free from all their suffering and to experience lasting peace and happiness. When we consider our present situation we see that at the moment, we don't actually have the power to do this but once we have become fully enlightened beings, we will have all kinds of abilities to help sentient beings get rid of their pains and problems and find peace and happiness.

## THE SUFFERING NATURE OF SAMSARA

If we reflect on the situation in which we find ourselves, we will realize that with so much unbearable pain and suffering, it is as though we were in a giant prison. This is the prison of cyclic existence. However, because of our distorted perception, we often see this prison as a very beautiful place; as if it were, in fact, a wonderful garden of joy. We don't really see what the disadvantages of samsara are, and because of this we find ourselves clinging to this existence. With this attachment, we continue creating karmic actions that precipitate our rebirth in it over and over again and thus keep us stuck in samsara.

If we look deep within ourselves, we find that it is the innate grasping at self that distorts our perception and makes us see cyclic existence as a pleasure land. All of us who are trapped in samsara share that kind of distorted perception, and as a result, we find ourselves creating all sorts of karmic actions. Even our good karmic actions are somewhat geared towards keeping us imprisoned within cyclic existence.

We should try to understand that being in cyclic existence is like being in a fire pit, with all the pain that such a situation would bring. When we understand this, we will start to change the nature of our karmic actions. Buddha said this in the sutras and Indian masters have carried this teaching over into the commentaries, or *shastras*. No matter where we live in samsara, we are bound to experience suffering. It doesn't matter with whom we live—our friends, family and companions all bring problems and suffering. Nor does it matter what kind of resources we have available to us; they too ultimately bring us pain and difficulty.

Now, you might think, "Well, that doesn't seem to be altogether true. In this world there are many wonderful places to visit—magnificent waterfalls, lovely wildernesses and so on. It doesn't seem as if samsara is such a bad place to be. Also, I have many wonderful friends who really care for me. It doesn't seem true that those in cyclic existence to whom I am close bring me problems and sufferings. Moreover, I have delicious food to eat and beautiful things to wear, so neither does it seem that everything I use in cyclic existence is suffering in nature." If such are our thoughts and feelings, then we have not realized the true nature of samsara, which is actually nothing but misery. Let me explain more about how things really are in samsara.

The first thing the Buddha spoke about after his enlightenment was the truth of suffering. There are three kinds of pains and problems in cyclic existence—the "suffering of misery," the "suffering of change" and "pervasive suffering." We can easily relate to the suffering of misery, as this includes directly manifested pain and problems, such as the pain we experience if we cut ourselves or get a headache. However, our understanding of suffering is usually limited to that. We don't generally perceive the misery of change, which is a subtler kind of suffering. Even when we experience some temporary pleasures and comforts in cyclic existence, we must understand that these things also change into pains and problems. Pervasive, or extensive, suffering is even more subtle and hence even more difficult for us to understand. Suffering is simply the nature of samsara. When we have a headache we take medicine for the pain or when there is a cut on our body we go to the doctor for treatment, but we generally don't seek treatment for the other two kinds of suffering.

Buddhas and bodhisattvas feel infinite compassion for those of us who are trapped within cyclic existence because we don't realize that our pain and suffering are our own creation. It is as though we are engaged in self-torture. Our suffering is due to our own negative karmic actions, which in turn are motivated by all sorts of deluded thoughts and afflictive emotions. Just as we would feel compassion for a close friend who had gone insane, so are the buddhas and

bodhisattvas constantly looking for ways in which to help us free ourselves from these problematic situations. With their infinite love and
compassion, they are always looking for ways to assist us in getting
out of this messy existence.

None of us would like to be a slave. Slaves go through all kinds of
altercations, restrictions and difficulties and try with all their might to
find freedom from their oppressors. Likewise, we have become slaves
to the oppressors of our own delusions and afflictive emotions. These
masters have enslaved us not only in this lifetime but for innumerable
lifetimes past. As a result, we have gone through countless pains and
sufferings in cyclic existence. Obviously, if we don't want to suffer
such bondage any longer, we need to make an effort at the first given
opportunity to try to free ourselves. In order to do this, we need to
cultivate the wisdom realizing selflessness, or emptiness. In Sanskrit,
the word is *shunyata,* or *tathata,* which is translated as "emptiness," or
"suchness." This wisdom is the only tool that can help us to destroy
the master of delusions—our self-grasping ignorance. Emptiness is
the ultimate nature of all that exists. As such it is the antidote with
which we can counteract all forms of delusion, including the root
delusions of ignorance, attachment and anger.

## THE SELF-CHERISHING ATTITUDE

Buddha has stated that for Mahayana practitioners, the self-cherishing attitude is like poison, whereas the altruistic, other-cherishing
attitude is like a wish-fulfilling gem. Self-centeredness is akin to a
toxic substance that we have to get out of our system in order to find
the jewel-like thought of cherishing other beings. When we ingest
poison it contaminates our body and threatens our very existence. In
the same way, the self-cherishing attitude ruins our chance to improve
our mind. With it, we destroy the possibility for enlightenment and
become harmful to others. By contrast, if we have the mental attitude
of cherishing other beings, not only will we be able to find happiness
and the best of everything we are seeking, but we will also be able to
bring goodness to others.

In order to cultivate the altruistic attitude, we should reflect on the kindness of all other beings. As we learn to appreciate their kindness we also learn to care for them. We might accept the general notion that sentient beings must be cherished, but when we come down to it we find ourselves thinking, "Well, so and so doesn't count because they have been mean or unpleasant to me, so I'll take them off the list and just help the rest." If we do that we are missing the whole point and are limiting our thinking. We need *all* other beings in order to follow the path that Buddha has shown us.

It is others who provide us with the real opportunities to grow spiritually. In fact, in terms of providing us with the actual opportunities to follow the path leading to enlightenment, sentient beings are just as kind to us as are the buddhas. To use a previous example in a different context, in order to grow any kind of fruit tree we need its seed. However, it's not enough just to have the seed—we also need good fertile soil, otherwise the seed won't germinate. So, although Buddha has given us the seed—the path to enlightenment—sentient beings constitute the field of our growth—the opportunities to actually engage in activities leading to the state of enlightenment.

PRACTICES FOR DEVELOPING BODHICITTA

There are two methods of instruction for developing bodhicitta. The first is the "six causes and one result," which has come down to us through a line of transmission from Shakyamuni Buddha to Maitreya and Asanga and his disciples. The second is called "equalizing and exchanging self for others," an instruction that has come down to us from Shakyamuni Buddha to Manjushri and Arya Nagarjuna and his disciples. It doesn't matter which of these two core instructions for developing bodhicitta we put into practice. The focal object of great compassion is all sentient beings and its aspect is wishing them to be free from every kind of pain and suffering.

We start at a very basic level. We try to cultivate compassion towards our family members and friends, then slowly extend our compassion to include people in our neighborhood, in the same country, on the same continent and throughout the whole world. Ultimately, we include within the scope of our compassion not only all people but all other beings throughout the universe. We find that we cannot cause harm to any sentient being because this goes against our compassion.

Before generating such compassion, however, we need to cultivate even-mindedness—a sense of equanimity towards others—because our compassion has to extend equally towards all sentient beings, without discrimination. Usually, we divide people mentally into different categories. We have enemies on one side, friends and relatives on another and strangers somewhere else. We react differently towards each group. We have very strong negative feelings towards our enemies—we put them way away from us and if anything bad happens to them we feel a certain satisfaction. We have an indifferent attitude towards those who are strangers—we don't care if bad or good things happen to them because to us, they don't count. But if anything happens to those near and dear to us, we are immediately affected and experience all kinds of feelings in response.

In order to balance our attitude towards people and other beings, we should understand that there is nothing fixed in terms of relationships between ourselves and others. Someone we now see as a very dear friend could become our worst enemy later on in this life or the next. Similarly, someone we regard as an enemy could become our best friend. When we take rebirth our relationships change. We may become someone of a different race or some kind of animal. There is so much uncertainty in this changing pattern of lives and futures. As we take this into consideration, we begin to realize that there's no sense in discriminating between friends and enemies. In the light of all this change we should understand that all beings should be treated equally.

As we train our minds in this way, the time will come when we feel as close to all sentient beings as we currently feel to our dearest relatives and friends. After balancing our attitude in regard to people and other beings, we will easily be able to cultivate great compassion. However, we should not confuse compassion with attachment. Some people, motivated by attachment to their own skill in helping or to the outcome of their assistance, become very close and helpful to others and think that this is compassion, but it is not. Great compassion is a quality that someone who hasn't yet entered the path of Mahayana could have. So, after cultivating compassion and bodhicitta, you should combine it with cultivating the wisdom that understands emptiness. This is known as "integrating method and wisdom" and is essential to reach the state of highest enlightenment.

I always qualify personal nirvana to differentiate it from enlightenment. In the higher practices, Theravadins cultivate a path that brings them to the state of nirvana, or liberation. These are people who are seeking personal freedom from cyclic existence. They talk about "liberation with remainder"—liberation that is attained while one still has the aggregates, the contaminated body and mind. "Liberation without remainder" means that one discards the body and then achieves the state of liberation. To attain the highest goal within the tradition of Theravada Buddhism, one has to observe pure ethics, study or listen to teachings on the practice, contemplate the teachings and then meditate on them. For those of us who are following the Mahayana tradition, however, our intention should be to do this work of enlightenment for the benefit and sake of all other sentient beings. In Mahayana Buddhist practice we also need to follow the same four steps, but we are not so much seeking our own personal goal as we are aspiring to become enlightened beings in order to be in a position to help others.

READINESS FOR RECEIVING EMPTINESS TEACHINGS

Mahayana Buddhism consists of two major categories or vehicles. The first is the Sutrayana, the Perfection Vehicle; the second is the Tantrayana, the Vajra Vehicle. In order for anyone to practice tantric Buddhism, he or she should be well prepared and should have become a suitable vessel for such teachings and practices. Sutrayana is more like an open teaching for everyone. However, there are exceptions to this rule.

Even within the Sutra Vehicle, the emptiness teachings should not be given to just anyone who asks but to only suitable recipients— those who have trained their minds to a certain point of maturity. Then, when the teachings on emptiness are given, they become truly beneficial to that person. Let's say that we have the seed of a very beautiful flower that we wish to grow. If we simply dump the seed into dry soil it is not going to germinate. This doesn't mean that there is something wrong with the seed. It's just that it requires other causes and conditions, such as fertile soil, depth and moisture in order to develop into a flower. In the same way, if a teaching on emptiness is given to someone whose mind is not matured or well-enough trained, instead of benefiting that person it could actually give them harm.

There was once a great Indian master named Drubchen Langkopa. The king of the region where he lived heard about this master and invited him to his court to give spiritual teachings. When Drubchen Langkopa responded to the king's request and gave a teaching on emptiness, the king went berserk. Although the master didn't say anything that was incorrect, the king completely misunderstood what was being taught because he wasn't spiritually prepared for it. He thought that the master was telling him that nothing existed at all. In his confusion, he decided that Drubchen Langkopa was a misleading guide and had him executed. Later on, another master was invited to the court. He gradually prepared the king for teachings on emptiness by first talking about the infallibility of the workings of the law of karmic actions and results, impermanence and so on. Finally, the king was ready to learn about emptiness as the ultimate reality and at last understood what it meant. Then he realized what a great mistake he had made in ordering the execution of the previous master.

This story tells us two things. Firstly, the teacher has to be very skillful and possess profound insight in order to teach emptiness to others. He or she needs two qualities known as "skillful means" and "wisdom." Secondly, the student needs to be ready to receive this teaching. The view of emptiness is extremely profound and is therefore hard to grasp. There are two aspects of emptiness, or selflessness—the emptiness, or selflessness, of the person and the emptiness, or selflessness, of phenomena.

People who are unprepared get scared that the teachings are actually denying the existence of everything. It sounds to them as if the teachings are rejecting the entire existence of phenomena. They don't understand that the term "emptiness" refers to the emptiness of *inherent*, or *true*, existence. They then take this misunderstanding and apply it to their own actions. They come to the conclusion that karmic actions and their results don't really exist at all and become wild and crazy, thinking that whatever makes their lives pleasurable or humorous is okay because their actions have no consequences.

Additionally, the listener's sense of ego can also become an obstacle, as the idea of emptiness can really frighten those who are not ready for it to the extent that they abandon their meditation on emptiness altogether. Buddha's teaching on emptiness is a core, or inner essence, teaching, and if for some reason we abandon it, this becomes a huge obstacle to our spiritual development. It is very important to remember that discovering the emptiness of any phenomenon is not the same as concluding that that phenomenon does not exist at all.

In his *Supplement to the Middle Way*, Chandrakirti describes indicative signs by which one can judge when someone is ready to learn about emptiness. He explains that just as we can assume that there is a fire because we can see smoke or that there is water because we can see water birds hovering above the land, in the same way, through certain external signs, we can infer that someone is ready to receive teachings on emptiness. Chandrakirti goes on to tell us, "When an ordinary being, on hearing about emptiness, feels great joy arising repeatedly within him and due to such joy, tears moisten his eye and the hair on his body stands up, that person has in his mind the seed for understanding emptiness and is a fit vessel to receive teachings on it."

If we feel an affinity for the teachings and are drawn towards them, it shows that we are ready. Of the external and internal signs, the internal are more important. However, if we don't have these signs, we should make strong efforts to make ourselves suitable vessels for teachings on emptiness. To do so, we need to do two things—accumulate positive energy and wisdom and purify our deluded, negative states of mind. For the sake of simplicity, we refer to these as the practices of *accumulation* and *purification*.

## ACCUMULATION

In order to achieve the two types of accumulation—the accumulation of merit, or positive energy, and the accumulation of insight, or wisdom—we can engage in the practice of the six perfections of generosity, ethics, patience, enthusiastic perseverance, concentration and wisdom. Through such practices we will be able to accumulate the merit and wisdom required for spiritual progress.

We can talk about three kinds of generosity (*dana,* in Sanskrit)—the giving of material things, the giving of Dharma and the giving of protection, or freedom from fear. The giving of material help is easily understood. In the *Lam-rim chen-mo,* Lama Tsong Khapa's great lam-rim text, we read that even if you have only a mouthful of food, you can practice material giving by sharing it with a really needy person. When we see homeless people on the streets, we often get irritated or frustrated by their presence. That is not a good attitude. Even if we can't give anything, we can at least wish that someday we will be in a position to help.

The giving of Dharma can be practiced by anyone, not just a lama. For example, when you do your daily practice with the wish to benefit others, there might be some divine beings or other invisible beings around you who are listening. So, when you dedicate your prayers to others, that is giving of Dharma, or spirituality. Somebody out there is listening; remember that. An example of giving protection would be saving somebody's life.

In his *Supplement,* Chandrakirti says, "They will always adopt pure ethics and observe them. They will give out of generosity, will cultivate compassion and will meditate on patience. Dedicating such virtue entirely to full awakening for the liberation of wandering beings, they pay respect to accomplished bodhisattvas."

In Tibetan, ethics, or moral discipline, is called *tsul-tim,* which means "the mind of protection." Ethics is a state of mind that protects us from negativity and delusion. For example, when we vow not to kill any sentient being, we develop the state of mind that protects us from the negativity of killing.

In Buddhism, we find different kinds of ethics. On the highest level there are the tantric ethics—tantric vows and commitments. At the level below these are the bodhisattva's ethics, and below these are the ethics for individual emancipation—*pratimoksha*, in Sanskrit.

If we want to practice Buddhism, then even if we have not taken the tantric or bodhisattva vows, there are still the ethics of the lay practitioner. And if we have not taken the lay vows, we must still observe the basic ethics of abandoning the ten negativities of body, speech and mind. Avoiding these ten negativities is the most basic practice of ethics. If anyone performs these ten actions, whether they are a Buddhist or not, they are committing a negativity.

There are three negativities of body—killing, stealing and indulging in sexual misconduct. There are four negativities of speech—lying, causing disharmony, using harsh language and indulging in idle gossip. There are three negativities of mind—harmful intent, covetousness and wrong, or distorted, views. When we develop the state of mind to protect ourselves from these negativities and thus cease to engage in them, we are practicing ethics. Furthermore, we must always try to keep purely any vows, ethics and commitments we have promised to keep.

In addition to these ten negativities there are also the five "boundless negativities," or heinous crimes. These are killing one's father, killing one's mother, killing an arhat, shedding the blood of an enlightened being—we use the term "shedding the blood" here because an enlightened being cannot be killed—and causing a schism in the spiritual community. These negativities are called "boundless" because after the death of anyone who has committed any of them, there is a very brief intermediate state followed immediately by rebirth directly into a bad migration such as the hell, hungry ghost or animal realms.

We have discussed generosity, ethics, patience and the need for enthusiasm and consistency in our practice. Regarding the remaining perfections of concentration and wisdom, even though we may not at present have a very high level of concentration, we do need to gain a certain amount of mental stability so that we don't indulge in negativities. We must also cultivate the perfection of wisdom, which understands the reality of emptiness. We may not yet have developed the wisdom that perceives emptiness as the ultimate nature of all phenomena, but we should begin by developing our "wisdom of discernment" so that we can differentiate between right and wrong actions and apply ourselves accordingly. All these things constitute the actual practice that can help us to attain good rebirths in future.

## PURIFICATION

We know that if we create any kind of karmic action—good, bad or neutral—we will experience its results. However, this does not mean that we cannot do anything to avoid the results of actions that we have already committed. If we engage in the practice of purification we can avoid having to experience the result of an earlier negative action. Some people believe that they have created too many negative actions to be able to transform themselves, but that's not true. The Buddha said that there isn't any negativity, however serious or profound, that cannot be changed through the practice of purification. Experienced masters say that the one good thing about negativities is that they can be purified. If we don't purify our mind, we cannot really experience the altruistic mind of enlightenment or the wisdom realizing emptiness.

As we look within ourselves, we find that we are rich with delusions. There are three fundamental delusions—the "three poisons" of ignorance, attachment and anger—which give rise to innumerable other delusions; as many as 84,000 of them. So, we have a lot of work to do to purify all these delusions as well as the negative karmic actions that we have created through acting under the influence of deluded motivation.

Let me tell you a true story from the life of Lama Tsong Khapa, who is believed to have been an emanation of Manjushri, the deity of wisdom. When Lama Tsong Khapa meditated on emptiness in the assembly of monks, he would become totally absorbed and simply rest in a non-dual state as if his mind and emptiness were one. After all the other monks had left the hall, Lama Tsong Khapa would still be sitting there in meditation. At times he would check his understanding of emptiness with Manjushri through the help of a mediator, a great master called Lama Umapa. Through this master, Lama Tsong Khapa once asked Manjushri, "Have I understood the view of emptiness exactly as presented by the great Indian Master, Nagarjuna?" The answer he received was "No." Manjushri advised Lama Tsong Khapa to go with a few disciples into intensive retreat and engage in purification and accumulation practices in order to deepen his understanding of emptiness.

In accordance with Manjushri's advice, Lama Tsong Khapa took eight close students, called the "eight pure disciples," and went to a place called Wölka, more than one hundred miles east of Lhasa. There, he and his students engaged in intensive purification and accumulation practices, including many preliminary practices such as full-length prostrations and recitation of the *Sutra of Confession to the Thirty-five Buddhas*. Lama Tsong Khapa did as many as 350,000 prostrations and made many more mandala offerings. When making this kind of offering, you rub the base of your mandala set with your forearm. Today, mandala sets are made of silver, gold or some other metal and are very smooth, but Lama Tsong Khapa used a piece of slate as his mandala base, and as a result of all his offerings wore the skin of his forearm raw.

We have a beautiful saying in Tibet: "The life-stories of past teachers are practices for posterity." So, when we hear about the lives of our lineage masters, they are not just stories but messages and lessons for us. The masters are telling us, "This is the way I practiced and went to the state beyond suffering."

During his retreat, Lama Tsong Khapa also read the great commentary to Nagarjuna's *Mulamadhyamaka* called *Root Wisdom*. Two lines of this text stood out for him—that everything that exists is characterized by emptiness and that there is no phenomenon that is not empty of inherent, or true, existence. It is said that at that very moment, Lama Tsong Khapa finally experienced direct insight into emptiness.

Some people think that emptiness isn't that difficult an insight to gain, but maybe now you can understand that it is not so easy. It is hard for many of us to sit for half an hour, even with a comfortable cushion. Those who are trained can sit for maybe forty minutes and if we manage to sit for a whole hour, we feel that it's marvelous. The great yogi Milarepa, on the other hand, did not have a cushion and sat so long that he developed calluses. This is a great teaching for us.

If masters or holy beings have created any negative karmic actions, they also have to experience their results unless those actions have been purified. Even those who are nearing enlightenment still have some things to purify and need to accumulate positive energy and wisdom. If this is true even for great masters and holy beings, then it must also be true for us. We have created innumerable negative karmic actions, so we should try to purify them as much as possible. All of us—old students, new students, and myself included—need to make as much effort as we can to purify our negativities, stop creating new ones and create more positive actions. This should be our practice. Many people might be doing their best to purify the negativities they have already accumulated but feel that they are not yet ready to completely stop creating more. As a result, they naturally get involved in negativities again. This is not good. You must do your best to both purify past negativities and not create any new ones.

The practice of purification, or confession, must include the "four opponent powers," or the "four powerful antidotes." The first opponent power is the "power of contrition," or regret. If we happen to accidentally drink some poison then we really regret it because we feel so terrible. This feeling motivates us to go for treatment to detoxify our body, but we also make a kind of commitment or determination not to make that same mistake again. So, we also need to generate what is known as the "power of resolution"—the firm determination not to repeat the negativity.

The other two opponent powers are the "power of the object of reliance" and the "power of the application of antidotes." Taking refuge in the Three Jewels and generating the altruistic mind of enlightenment constitutes the power of reliance. Cultivating any general or specific meditation practice (such as meditation on the equality of self and others) constitutes the power of the application of the antidote. There is no negativity that can stand up to these four opponent powers.

# THREE

# MIND TRAINING, DEVELOPING EMPTINESS

## THE WISDOM THAT PERCEIVES EMPTINESS

We have already dealt with training our mind in cultivating conventional bodhicitta, or the conventional mind of enlightenment. We now need to look at how to cultivate ultimate bodhicitta—the mind of enlightenment that deals with emptiness. The mind training text we are studying presents actual instructions for cultivating the ultimate awakening mind. In certain texts such as this one, you will find that the conventional mind of enlightenment is presented first and followed by the ultimate mind of enlightenment. In other texts, the order of presentation is reversed. The reason has to do with the mental faculties of Mahayana practitioners. For those with sharp faculties, emptiness is presented first. For those with relatively less sharp faculties the conventional truth is taught before the ultimate.

There are four major traditions within Tibetan Buddhism—Gelug, Kagyu, Nyingma and Sakya. We may find differences between them in terminology or the emphasis of certain practices, but they are all authentic Buddhist traditions. The Kagyu and Gelug traditions use the term *mahamudra*—"The Great Seal"—to talk about emptiness, whereas the Nyingmapas use the term *dzog-chen*—"The Great Perfection"—to refer to the same thing. In the Nyingma tradition, there is a tantric practice called *atiyoga*, which means the pinnacle, or topmost, vehicle. This could be compared to *dzog-rim*, the completion stage practice of the Gelug tradition, which is the most exalted practice of highest yoga tantra.

When people hear about The Great Perfection of the Nyingmapas they may think that this tradition has something that other Tibetan Buddhist traditions do not, but this is not the case. Each of these traditions is talking about the ultimate nature or reality, which we also call the profound Middle View, or Middle Way. Also, some people might think that because dzog-rim practice is said to be very profound, it must be a quick and easy way to reach enlightenment without having to do meditation. It is never like that. Meditation is as essential in Tantrayana as it is in Sutrayana. It's not as if in tantric practice you just do some rituals, ring the bell—ding! ding! ding!—and then you get enlightened. No; you have to meditate.

As the great Atisha tells us, the way to conduct one's studies of meditation and contemplation in order to realize the true nature of emptiness is by following the instructions of Nagarjuna's disciple, Chandrakirti. Lama Tsong Khapa elucidates the view of emptiness in accordance with the system of Arya Nagarjuna and Chandrakirti. It is within Lama Tsong Khapa's mind-stream that we find the presence of the buddhas of the three times, and I am going to explain emptiness in accordance with Lama Tsong Khapa's way.

WHY DID THE BUDDHA TEACH EMPTINESS?

The historical Buddha, Shakyamuni, taught the profound middle path—the way of the wisdom perceiving emptiness, or selflessness—in order to liberate us from samsara. It is by way of perceiving and experiencing emptiness that we will be able to counteract our basic sense of ignorance, or grasping at self.

There is a passage from the sutras: "Thus, not being able to realize that which is known as emptiness, peaceful and unproduced, sentient beings have been helplessly wandering in different states of cyclic existence. Seeing this, the enlightened one has revealed, or established, emptiness through hundred-fold reasoning." What this tells us is that we ordinary sentient beings, who are unable to see the ultimate nature of everything that exists, create all kinds of negative karmic actions for ourselves and face unwanted problems and sufferings as a result. All the teachings Buddha gave either directly or indirectly point to what emptiness is. This is because the sole purpose of

Buddha's teaching is to free all of us from the causes of suffering.

## TRUTH AND FORM BODIES

For us to reach the state of enlightenment we need to understand the basis, the path and the result. The basis consists of the two truths, the conventional truth and the ultimate truth. The path is method and wisdom, or skillful means and awareness. The result consists of the two enlightened bodies—the form body, or rupakaya, and the truth body, or dharmakaya. First we must study the view of emptiness as presented by enlightened beings. This is our basis. Then, as trainees on the path, we need to integrate method and wisdom. We must never separate method and wisdom from one another. If we focus on one and forget the other, we are going to get stuck. Eventually, as a result of this practice, each of us will reach the enlightened state and be able to realize the form body and the truth body.

Although nominally different from each other, these enlightened bodies actually share the same nature. For example, Avalokiteshvara, whom Tibetans call Chenrezig, can manifest in innumerable ways to work for sentient beings, yet all these manifestations are Avalokiteshvara. When we become buddhas we will do so in the form of the buddhas of the five families, the five dhyani buddhas. So, you may ask, what happens when I become a buddha, a completely awakened being? Having actualized the form and truth bodies, you will be working solely to help others become free from cyclic existence. You will be constantly working for their benefit until samsara is empty of all sentient beings.

The primary cause for accomplishing the enlightened form body is the practice of method, the collection of positive energy, or merit. The primary cause for accomplishing the truth body is the collection of wisdom, or insight, particularly the wisdom realizing emptiness. This does not mean that accumulating either merit or wisdom alone will allow us to reach the state of enlightenment. When we understand that the wisdom realizing emptiness is the primary cause for the truth body, implicitly we should understand that in order to accomplish that body we must practice method as well.

## THE MUTUAL DEPENDENCE OF SUBJECT AND OBJECT

Everything that exists can be classified into objects or subjects. There isn't any phenomenon that doesn't belong to one of these two categories. However, object and subject—the observed and the observer—are actually mutually dependent upon one another. If there is no object, there cannot be an observer of that object. This is what Chandrakirti states in his *Supplement to the Middle Way*: "Without an object, one cannot establish its perceiver."

There is a line from the mind training text that says, "Consider all phenomena as like a dream." This does not mean that everything that exists *is* a dream, but that it can be compared to a dream. If you miss this emphasis, then when you read in the *Heart Sutra*, "no ear, no nose, no tongue" and so forth, you will interpret this passage to mean that those things don't exist at all, which is a totally bizarre notion. This is the position of the nihilist—someone who rejects even the *conventional* existence of phenomena. We know that the things in our dreams don't really exist, that they are dependent upon our mind. Also, for us to experience a dream, the necessary causes and conditions must come together. First we have to sleep, but if we go into a very deep sleep then we're not going to dream. Just as a dream occurs as a result of certain causes and conditions, such is the case with everything that exists. Every functional phenomenon depends upon causes and conditions for its existence. This is a fact of reality. Nothing exists in and of itself, inherently, or objectively. Everything exists *dependently*, that is, in dependence upon its parts, and so we say that things are *empty* of inherent, or objective, existence.

The next line in the stanza reads: "Analyze the nature of unborn/unproduced awareness." What this means is that this subjective mind, or consciousness, is not born or produced inherently, in and of itself. As much as objective phenomena are to be seen like dreams, which arise from their causes and conditions and are empty of inherent existence, subjective phenomena, too, exist dependently and are empty of inherent existence. We must analyze the non-inherent nature of our awareness, or mind.

With the line, "Consider all phenomena like a dream," we are primarily dealing with the observed, or the object. When we discuss awareness we shift our focus onto the observer, or the subject. If you perceive that objects don't exist independently, or inherently, then what about their subjects? Do they exist inherently? Again, the answer is no. Just like the object, the subject does not exist inherently, in and of itself. Just as objects and their perception exist dependently, so does the person who is experiencing and interacting with the objects and perceptions. The observed and the observer are both empty of inherent existence.

## INTELLECTUAL AND INNATE FORMS OF IGNORANCE

Ignorance is the grasping at inherent existence, especially the inherent existence of the self. There are two forms, the intellectual and the innate. The intellectual form of ignorance—grasping at the inherent existence of "I," or self—is found in those whose minds have been affected by some kind of philosophical ideas, but the innate form exists in the mind of every sentient being.

The type of grasping at inherent existence that is presented in the *Abhidharmakosha,* the *Treasury of Knowledge,* and its commentaries is the intellectual form. If this were to be taken as the root cause of samsara, then our position would have to be that only those whose minds have been influenced by philosophical concepts could possess the root cause of cyclic existence. According to this view, birds and other animals couldn't have this cause of cyclic existence because they can't study or be influenced by philosophy. It is certainly true that yaks and goats don't sit around discussing philosophy, so they don't have the intellectual form of grasping at self. However, the root cause of samsara exists in the mind-streams of *all* sentient beings who are trapped in cyclic existence.

The text provides a quote from the *Supplement to the Middle Way* to clarify this point. "Even those who have spent many eons as animals and have not beheld an unproduced or permanent self are seen to be involved in the misconception of an I." What this passage is telling us is that beings who remain in the animal realm for many lifetimes do not possess the intellectual grasping at self but they do have the innately developed form of ignorance. Therefore, the root cause of cyclic existence cannot be intellectual but must be the innately, or spontaneously, developed ignorant conception that grasps at the self.

## INNATE IGNORANCE IS THE ROOT OF CYCLIC EXISTENCE

We need to ask ourselves what the original root cause of cyclic existence is. How did we get here in the first place? Having discovered this cause, we can then apply the method to counteract it. Due to our ignorant attachment to self, we grasp at and get attached to everything that we perceive as being ours and at anything that we think will help to make us happy. This is the root delusion. When we discuss the process of coming into and getting out of cyclic existence—taking rebirth and becoming liberated—we talk about what are known as the twelve links of interdependent origination. In the mind training text, there is a quote that spells out three of these twelve links, which are the main reasons we remain in samsara.

Our innate self-grasping ignorance is the root cause of samsara, so ignorance is the first link. It is because of this ignorance that we create karmic actions, therefore the second link is called karmic formation. This refers not only to bad karmic actions but also includes positive and neutral ones as well. These karmic actions then deposit their latencies upon our consciousness, or mind-stream. Our minds carry the imprints of all the good and bad karmic actions we have created, and when any of these karmic imprints get activated, they can precipitate all the other links and lead to our rebirth either in either a positive or a negative state.

There are six types of sentient beings in cyclic existence. Of these six, three are relatively fortunate types of rebirth and three are unfortunate. Under the influence of ignorance we could create positive karmic actions and, as a result, take one of the good rebirths as a human being, a demigod (*asura*) or a god (*sura*). For a positive karmic action to lead to a fortunate rebirth it must be activated by positive conditions. However, even someone who takes a good rebirth is still bound to cyclic existence.

Similarly, under the influence of the delusions of ignorance, attachment or aversion we might create negative karmic actions. These leave imprints on our mental consciousness such that when they are activated by other negative actions or conditioning factors, we can be reborn in one of the three bad migrations. Great negativities precipitate rebirth in the hells. Negativities of medium intensity precipitate rebirth as a hungry ghost. Small negativities can still cause us to be reborn in the lower realms as some kind of animal.

Karmic formations connect us to our next conception in our mother's womb, which is the tenth dependent link of existence. These three links of ignorance, karmic actions and existence are very important. To substantiate this point we have a quote from Arya Nagarjuna's *Seventy Stanzas on Emptiness*, "Actions are caused by disturbing emotions." In other words, the karmic actions we create can be traced back to our innate self-grasping, which is the origin of our disturbing emotions, or delusions. Nagarjuna continues, "Karmic formations have a disturbed nature and the body is caused by karmic actions. So, all three are empty of their own entity." This means that because ignorance, karmic formations and existence all interact with one another to cause our rebirth, they are therefore all empty of inherent existence.

We should train ourselves to clearly ascertain the way in which we enter cyclic existence because then we can work to reverse this process. Once we have put an end to our delusions and contaminated karmic actions we will achieve the state of liberation. This is what Nagarjuna refers to in his *Fundamental Wisdom Treatise* when he says, "You are liberated when your delusions and contaminated karmic actions are exhausted." We must all understand that any situation we go through is nothing but our own creation—the results of our karmic actions. Usually when things go wrong we find someone else to blame as if others were responsible for our wellbeing. If we can't find other fellow beings to blame then we blame inanimate objects like food. Either way, we always view ourselves as pure and separate from things.

Again, we can use the example of a seed to understand karma. If the seed is not there in the first place, then even if all the other conditions needed for growth are present, we are not going to see any fruit.

In the same way, if we ourselves do not create any good or bad karmic actions, conditioning factors alone cannot bring us any good or bad results. However, once we have created these actions, they can be activated or ripened by other conditions. It is in that sense that other people can act as conditioning factors to activate our good and bad karmic actions. Even the kind of food we eat can be a conditioning factor to activate certain karmic actions we have created. Even so, it is the karmic actions themselves that are the most important factor in bringing good and bad situations upon us. We should adopt positive actions and abandon negative ones because it is us who will experience their results. We should feel that every good and bad experience is the result of our own seed-like karmic actions. This is a very good subject for meditation.

We should understand that the ignorance of grasping at self, which all of us have within our mind-stream, is the very ignorance that locks us like a jailer within the walls of samsara. In the diagram of the wheel of life, which depicts the twelve dependent links, a blind person represents ignorance. We are blind with regard to what we need to abandon in our lives—to what we should not be doing—and also blind to what we need to cultivate in our lives—to what we should be doing. Just as an untrained blind person will create a big mess around himself or herself, so we make a mess of our lives. And we continue doing this, repeating the whole process of samsara and perpetuating a cycle that is very difficult to stop.

We all wish for happiness, but the happiness that we experience is very small. We don't want any kind of pain or problem, but innumerable pains and problems befall us. Deep down we are motivated by the ignorance of grasping at self and engage in different kinds of karmic actions, which bring forth all kinds of experiences. The wisdom that realizes selflessness is the direct antidote to our ignorant self-grasping.

All of us who want to reach the state of highest enlightenment must combine the practice of the two aspects of the path—skillful means, the extensive aspect of the path, and wisdom, the profound aspect of the path—as presented by the two great pioneers of Buddhadharma, Arya Asanga and Arya Nagarjuna respectively. First, we must recognize that the innate ignorance of self-grasping is the root cause of cyclic existence, or samsara. Then we have to deal with the presentation of selflessness, or emptiness, which is the antidote to this ignorance. The Tibetan word, *rig-pa*, literally means "to see," and *ma-rig-pa* means "to not see." Ma-rig-pa is translated as "ignorance" while rig-pa is translated as "wisdom." In other words, wisdom directly opposes, or counteracts, ignorance. Rig-pa doesn't just mean any kind of awareness or wisdom—it refers specifically to the awareness, or wisdom, that realizes emptiness.

## GRASPING AT SELF AND PHENOMENA

There are two kinds of objects of this ignorant grasping—the grasping at the self of persons and the grasping at the self of phenomena. Both kinds of grasping are misconceptions because the focus of both is non-existent. The grasping at the self of persons means perceiving a person to exist inherently and objectively. This grasping is an active misconception because it is projecting something that doesn't actually exist. The self does not exist in and of itself—it is not inherently existent—however, our innate self-grasping *perceives* the self, or I, to exist in that manner. Our self-grasping, or ego-grasping, (*dag-dzin* in Tibetan) actually serves to fabricate the way that the self appears to exist for us. Similarly, grasping at the self of phenomena means that a person perceives phenomena to exist inherently and objectively. There isn't a self of phenomena but our grasping makes one up. It exaggerates and fabricates a self of phenomena and then grasps at its supposed inherent reality. So, we can talk about two kinds of selflessness, the selflessness of a person and the selflessness of phenomena. When we refute the inherent existence of a person, we are dealing with the selflessness of a person, but when we refute the inherent existence of anything else we are dealing with the selflessness of phenomena.

What we mean by "a person" is a projection, or label, that is placed onto the collection of someone's five physical and mental aggregates of form, feeling, discriminative awareness, conditioning factors and consciousness. When we take a person as our basis of investigation and think that this person exists in and of himself or herself, that is what is called "grasping at the self of a person." If we grasp at the inherent existence of the aggregates, that is, at any part of a person, whether it be a part of body or mind, that is called "grasping at the self of phenomena." This is described as including all things from "form to omniscient mind." In Nagarjuna's *Precious Garland*, it is stated, "So long as the aggregates are misconceived, an I is misconceived upon them. If we have this conception of an I, then there is action that results in birth." What this passage is saying is that as long as we grasp at the physical and mental constituents, or aggregates, as being truly and inherently existent, then we will have the misconception of a truly existent I. Due to this grasping we create karmic actions that precipitate our rebirth and cause us to become trapped again and again within cyclic existence.

The object of our grasping at the self of a person is an inherently existing self. This is something that doesn't exist at all, yet our grasping makes it feel as if that kind of self truly exists and we cling to it in this way. Similarly, the object of the grasping at the self of phenomena is an inherently existent self of phenomena. From these two innate forms of grasping come attachment to the happiness of I. Attachment to one's own happiness actually depends upon the concept of "my" and "mine"—my feelings, my possessions, my body, my family etc. As Chandrakirti states in *Supplement to the Middle Way*, "At first there arises the conception of and attachment to I, or self, and then there arises the conception of and attachment to mine." We experience the grasping at the self of a person, and this grasping then induces the grasping at the self of phenomena, which is the grasping at mine. Due to the strength of our clinging to these feelings of I, my and mine, we are not able to see the fallacy of seeking self-happiness. This attachment obscures our mind and we are unable to see what is wrong with it.

From being attached to ourselves we become so attached to our things and different parts of our bodies that some of us even change our appearance through plastic surgery. If we weren't attached to our I, we could be totally liberated and free, like Milarepa. He turned a strange greenish color from eating nettles, but this didn't matter to him because he wasn't attached to his appearance. As we look into this mirror of teaching, we can see a different kind of reflection of ourselves—one that shows us how we grasp at things and how attachment arises within us.

It is important for us to understand that "I" and "mine" are not identical. If we can't differentiate between these two, we will have problems later on. The object of our innate grasping at self is the "I" not the "mine," because mine includes the physical and mental aggregates. Chandrakirti explains that if the aggregates of the person were the object of our innate grasping at the self of a person, then we should be able to perceive our aggregates as being I, which we are not able to do. Also, if the aggregates are taken to be the self, then we have to assert that there are five selves because there are five aggregates. The kind of conception that arises with regard to the aggregates is not the conception of I but the conception of mine. We do not think about our ears or our nose as our self, but as things belonging to our self. In the same way, when we investigate our mind, we don't find any part that is I.

We should examine, investigate and analyze the mode of apprehension of our innate grasping at self. In other words, how does our innate grasping perceive the self to exist? What does our innate ignorance perceive? What does it grasp at? We should always focus upon our own condition and not point our finger at someone else's ignorance. Having discovered this, we must then find the means of generating a different kind of perception, one that directly contradicts the mistaken one that grasps at self. This perception is the perfect view of emptiness, or selflessness. However, in order to realize this view, we first have to be clear about what this view actually is. We need to establish the correct view of emptiness.

USING A BASIS TO DESCRIBE EMPTINESS

There is no way to reveal emptiness nakedly or directly because we must use words and terminology. It is only through conventional terms that emptiness can be revealed. In other words, there is no way to discuss emptiness without using something as a basis. For example, when we talk about the emptiness of forms, these forms constitute the basis upon which their emptiness is then established. This is also the case with any other phenomenon—sound, smell, taste and so forth. Everything around us is characterized by emptiness and so our body or any other phenomenon constitutes the basis upon which we can then understand its emptiness.

In the *Heart Sutra* we read that "Form is emptiness and emptiness is form." This means that the ultimate nature of form is emptiness and that emptiness relates to form. Emptiness is not the same as form, but in order to understand emptiness we have to take form into consideration as our focal object. Without dealing with a form, we cannot understand its emptiness. There is a line of a prayer that states, "The wisdom gone beyond (emptiness) is beyond words and expression." The Tibetan translation suggests that it is also beyond thought. This means that without depending upon a basis you cannot even conceptualize what emptiness is.

The same thing is stated by Arya Nagarjuna in his *Root Wisdom Treatise*, where we read, "Without depending upon conventional terms or terminology, one cannot reveal the ultimate truth or reality." When we deal with emptiness, however, it may have nothing to do with form at all. In certain mental states, for example, we don't perceive forms; for instance, when we are in a deep sleep. Even so, it is empty.

When we deal with the selflessness of a person, the basis for that selflessness is the person. Therefore, it is in relation to the person that we establish the person's emptiness. When we deal with a person's aggregates (body, feelings, thoughts, perceptions and so forth), we are dealing with a different kind of basis, one that is the selflessness of phenomena. The text tells us that with regard to what is being refuted, there is no difference in subtlety between establishing the selflessness of a person and establishing the selflessness of phenomena. So, once we understand the selflessness of a person, we don't have to repeat our reasoning over again to understand the selflessness of phenomena. We can simply shift our focus onto another object while remembering the same reasoning with which we realized the selflessness of a person. This is what the great Indian master Aryadeva was saying in his *Four Hundred Stanzas on the Middle View* when he stated, "The view of an object is the view of everything else."

## THE OBJECT OF NEGATION, OR REFUTATION

In order to realize what selflessness or emptiness is, we must first understand its opposite. What is the antithesis of selflessness? What is it that we are trying to refute, or negate, in order to establish what emptiness is? What we are refuting is the way that our innate self-grasping perceives the self as existing truly, inherently and objectively. Therefore, we say that inherent, objective or true existence of the self is the "object of refutation" or the "object of negation." The object of refutation, or negation, is the thing that we are denying exists.

There are a few terms that may sound different from one another but which, in the context of Prasangika-Madhyamaka (the school of philosophy that we are studying here), all mean the same thing. They are "existing by way of its own characteristic," "existing from its own side," "existing in and of itself," "inherent existence," "objective existence", "independent existence" and "true existence." Also, the terms "I," "self" and "person" all mean the same thing.

We can speak about the object of refutation on two levels—the object of refutation by reasoning and the object of refutation by scriptural authority. Inherent existence is the object of refutation by one's own valid reasoning, because nothing exists in and of itself without being imputed by terms and concepts. The object of refutation according to scriptural authority, however, is the *grasping* at that object, such as the grasping at the inherent, or true, existence of the self. Even though it is an object of refutation, that grasping actually does exist. There is no inherently existent self; however, there is grasping at the self's inherent existence as if it existed inherently. Therefore, the object of refutation by reasoning (inherent existence) refers to something that does not exist, but the object of refutation according to scriptural authority (grasping at inherent existence) refers to something that does exist.

Let us say that we want to investigate the emptiness of a particular form, such as a vase. As we analyze the vase, we must remember that we cannot perceive its emptiness by negating its very existence. Perceiving the vase's emptiness is not the same as concluding that the vase does not exist at all. If we refute, or negate, the conventional existence of the vase, then we have fallen into the extreme position of the nihilist. We have annihilated the vase's very existence and, as a result, we are not going to discover its emptiness. So, if we are not refuting the conventional or nominal existence of form in our search for emptiness, what is it that we *are* refuting? What is it that doesn't really exist? What we are refuting and what does not exist is the *inherent existence* of form. If we want to hit a target with an arrow we need to be able to see exactly where that target is. In the same way, to understand what emptiness is, we must be able to precisely identify what it is that is being refuted.

## REFUTING TOO MUCH AND NOT REFUTING ENOUGH

If we overestimate the object of negation then we will be refuting too much, but if we underestimate the object of negation we won't be refuting enough. An example of refuting too much is when we take conventional existence and inherent existence to be one and the same, concluding that because phenomena don't exist inherently they must not exist at all. When we take this position we are denying the existence of everything and have become nihilists. Remember, conventional existence and true existence do not mean the same thing.

If we deny the existence of everything then we won't be able to assert the distinction between the two types of phenomena—deluded phenomena (which includes our contaminated karmic actions and delusions, or afflictive emotions) and the liberated aspect of phenomena (which includes the spiritual paths, the true cessation of suffering and so forth). We won't be able to talk about the infallible law of karmic actions and their results because we will be asserting that its existence is merely a hallucination. If we cannot present the existence of both contaminated and uncontaminated phenomena, then we cannot present the complete structure of the path leading to spiritual liberation.

On the other hand, if we underestimate the object of negation and don't refute enough, that is as much of a problem as refuting too much. Certain schools of Buddhism assert only the selflessness of a person and not the selflessness of phenomena. Other schools assert both types of selflessness. Within each of the four schools of Buddhist thought—Vaibhashika, Sautrantika, Cittamatra and Madhyamaka—we find sub-schools. In the Madhyamaka, or Middle Way, school we find two major sub-schools, the Svatantrika-Madhyamaka, or Inference Validators, and the Prasangika-Madhyamaka, or Consequentialists. The Prasangika-Madhyamaka school's presentation of emptiness is considered the most authentic and it is this presentation that we are studying. The schools of Vaibhashika, Sautrantika, Cittamatra and Svatantrika-Madhyamaka all present an assertion of deluded states of mind that we find in Jamgon Kongtrul Yonten Gyatso's *Treasury of Knowledge*, the root text of which is the *Abhidharmakosha*.

The Prasangika-Madhyamaka school, however, presents in addition to these delusions, a subtle form of delusion that the other schools have not been able to identify—the conceptual grasping at inherent existence. Except for the Prasangika-Madhyamaka, all the other Buddhist schools assert the inherent existence of phenomena. They assert that if things don't exist inherently, they can't exist at all. The Svatantrika-Madhyamikas, who are in the same school as the Prasangikas, make a distinction between the *true* existence of phenomena and the *inherent* existence of phenomena. They say that things do exist inherently, from their own side, but that they do not exist truly. Their explanation for this distinction is that things exist from their own side *as well as* being posited by thought, or concept. According to them, a phenomenon exists as a *combination* of existence from its own side and of the mental thought imputed onto it. They don't include the conceptual grasping at inherent existence as a subtle delusion. Therefore, the Svatantrika-Madhyamaka and other Buddhist schools, apart from the Prasangika-Madhyamaka, have not been able to refute enough in order to establish selflessness or emptiness. In other words, the object of negation identified in their schools is inadequate.

There are many people who try to meditate on emptiness, but I believe that those who really know such meditation are very few. If you overestimate the object of negation and refute too much, you are off track, and if you underestimate the object of negation and don't refute enough, you again miss the point. It's like a mathematical

equation. The text cautions us that we have to be very precise in identifying what is to be refuted and refute exactly that amount—no
more and no less.

## HOW INNATE IGNORANCE PERCEIVES SELF AND PHENOMENA

We have seen how the innate form of ignorance is the root cause of
our being in samsara, therefore, we must study how this ignorance
perceives or apprehends its object, be it a person, a person's thoughts
or a physical thing. Naturally, ignorance apprehends its object in a
distorted way, yet how exactly does our innate ignorance perceive
things? It perceives things to exist in and of themselves, from their
own side, by way of their own characteristics and without being
imputed by terms and concepts. However, this is not the way in
which things actually exist. In fact, this kind of existence is a complete fabrication.

There is a popular Tibetan children's story that illustrates this
point. A lion was always bothering a rabbit, so the rabbit began to
plan a way to get rid of him. The rabbit went to the lion and said, "I
have seen another beast even more ferocious than you." The lion was
outraged by this notion because he felt that he was the king of all the
animals. The rabbit said, "Come with me, I'll show you," and took
the lion to a lake and told him to look into the water. The lion looked
carefully into the water and when he saw his own reflection, he
thought it was actually another lion. He bared his teeth at his own
reflection but it did exactly the same thing back at him from the
water. The rabbit said, "You see that dangerous animal down there?
He is the one who is more ferocious than you and if you don't kill
him, you won't be the strongest guy in the forest." The lion became
even angrier and jumped right into the water. He struggled and
splashed for a while but could not find the other lion, so he crawled
out onto the bank. The poor lion looked really confused and bedrag-
gled, but the rabbit, laughing to himself, said, "I think you didn't dive
deep enough; try again." So, the lion went even deeper into the lake
and eventually drowned trying to fight with his own reflection.

We have seen that the ignorance of self-grasping is of two kinds—

an intellectual form and an innately developed form, and we have established that it is the innate ignorance, the innate self-grasping, that is the root cause of all our problems. So, how does this innate form of ignorance perceive or grasp at I? Without knowing this, even if we try to engage in analytical meditation on selflessness we will never understand it. If a thief has run into a forest, his footprints will be in the forest. If we look for his footprints in the meadow, we will never find the thief.

Also, we must have a clear idea or picture of what inherent or self-existence is. If the I *were* inherently existent then how would it exist? Until we can precisely identify the inherent existence of I, we will never be able to realize the absence of the inherently existing I, that is selflessness. It is for that reason that the great bodhisattva, Shantideva, states in his *Guide to the Bodhisattva's Way of Life*, or *Bodhisattva-caryavatara*, that until you identify the object of grasping at true existence you won't be able to understand its non-existence; its lack of inherent, or true, existence. Therefore, we need to make a great deal of effort to identify how the I appears to our innate form of ignorance. It is relatively easy for us to understand that we do have this innate grasping at our self but we have difficulty seeing exactly *how* this grasping perceives the I to exist. Once we are sure that we have found the object of refutation, then in order to realize what emptiness is, we have to refute that object.

We all know that snow is white but it is possible that someone with certain sensory defects will perceive snow as yellow. That is an example of a distorted perception that misconceives the true color of snow. In a similar way, our grasping at self is a distorted perception that misconceives the self to exist in and of itself. The valid perception of snow as white invalidates the perception of snow as yellow. In the same way, our grasping at I is invalidated by the wisdom that perceives selflessness. When we actualize and experience this wisdom, then the grasping at self must leave because we understand that the way in which the self actually exists is the opposite of the way that our self-grasping perceived it.

Through this reasoning, we are trying to establish that the self could not exist in and of itself. As we refute the inherent existence of

I, what we are establishing on the other hand is selflessness. If the self does not exist inherently, then how does it exist? It exists being empty of inherent existence. This is how we establish selflessness. We will deal with this topic from different perspectives and angles so that we can really understand it.

The self is apprehended as existing objectively, in and of itself. The example given in the text is a person who is completely ignorant about the fact that the reflection of a face in the mirror is not the real face. Like the lion in the story, such a person cannot tell what is real from what is not real.

## WHAT IS SELF?

When someone calls you by your name, by the time you respond there is some kind of concept or picture of yourself that has emerged in your mind. You may not get a very clear or lucid concept of this self, but you do experience some kind of rough imagery of yourself before you answer. This self is something that seems to exist independently of anything else. It's a sort of solid point, a fixed entity that is just there by itself. It's very important for each of us to personally find out where this image of self or concept of I comes from. Does it come from the collection of our body and mind? Or does it come from a single part of our body or mind?

If an I exists then we should be able to find it within either our body or our mind. We have to analyze each part to find where the sense, concept, or image of I comes from. Let's say that your name is John. Who or what is John? You should investigate from the hair of your head down to your toes whether or not any particular part of your body is John. When you have eliminated one part, go on to the next. Then do the same kind of analytical meditation on your mind.

Like your body, your mind also has many parts, so you should try to find out whether any one part of the mind can be identified as I. There are many levels or kinds of mind and every one has its preceding and subsequent moments. You have to look at every minor detail and ask yourself, "Is this moment responsible for the sense of I?" Westerners love to do research; this is a good topic to research. If you feel that your concept or image of I comes out of a particular part of yourself, be it body or mind, then that is what you identify as being your self. You might think, for example, that your sense of I comes from your brain. However, because each aspect of your body and mind has multiple parts, then logically, you must have that many I's or selves within you. Mind is a whole world in itself, with many states and levels. So which one is the self?

At the end of your analytical meditation, you will not be able to pinpoint any part of your body and mind as being an inherently existent I. At this point you might get scared because you haven't found yourself. You may feel that you've lost your sense of identity. There is a vacuity—an absence of something. However, when you really develop certitude of the absence of an inherent I, you should then simply try to remain in that state of meditation as long as you can. As your understanding of the absence of self improves, then outside your meditation sessions you will be able to realize that although the self seemed to exist inherently, this perception was simply the result of your innate grasping. Next time someone calls your name, try to do this examination.

The mind training text states that when we investigate how our innate conception of I apprehends the self to exist, we must make sure that our investigation is not mixed up with the intellectual grasping at self. The text reads, "Detailed recognition of this comes about through cultivating a close relationship with a spiritual friend of the Great Vehicle and pleasing him for a long time." Thus, if we want to comprehend every detail and subtlety of this issue, it is essential that we consistently rely upon a qualified Mahayana guide.

DEPENDENT ARISING

At the end of your analysis it may seem as though no conventional realities or phenomena exist, including the law of karmic actions and results. However, they do exist—they just don't exist in the way that you thought they did. They exist *dependently*; that is, their existence depends upon certain causes and conditions. Therefore, we say that phenomena are "dependently arising." All the teachings of Buddha are based upon the principle of the view of dependent arising. As Lama Tsong Khapa states in his *Three Principal Paths*, "…it eliminates the extreme of eternalism." This means that because things appear to your perceptions to exist only conventionally or nominally, their true, or inherent, existence is eliminated. The next line says, "…it eliminates the extreme of nihilism." So, when you understand emptiness you will be able to eliminate the idea of complete non-existence. You will understand that it is not that things are completely non-existent, it is just that they exist dependently. They are dependent arisings.

In Arya Nagarjuna's *Root Wisdom Treatise*, he says that there isn't any phenomenon that is not dependently existent, therefore there isn't any phenomenon that is not empty of independent, or inherent, existence. Dependent arising is what we use to establish emptiness. Everything exists by depending upon something else, therefore everything is empty of inherent existence. When we use the valid reasoning of dependent arising we can find the emptiness of everything that exists. For example, by understanding that the self is dependently arising, we establish the selflessness of a person.

An example we could use is the reflection of our own face in the mirror. We all know that the reflection is not the real face, but how is it produced? Does it come just from the glass, the light, the face? Our face has to be there, but there also has to be a mirror, enough light for us to see and so on. Therefore, we see the reflection of our face in the mirror as a result of several things interacting with one another. We can investigate the appearance of our self to our perception in the same way. The self appears to us, but where does this appearance come from? Just like the reflection of the face in a mirror, it is an example of dependent arising.

This is quite clear in the case of functional things such as produced, or composite, phenomena, but there are other phenomena that are not produced by causes and conditions. However, they too exist dependently, that is, through mutual dependence upon other factors. For example, in the *Precious Garland*, Nagarjuna talks about how the descriptive terms of "long" and "short" are established through mutual comparison. "If there exists something that is long, then there would be something that is short." This kind of existence is dependently arising, but it is not dependent upon causes and conditions. So, dependent arising can mean several things. As we practice analytical meditation on emptiness we need to bring these different meanings into our meditation.

Dependent arising also refers to how everything is imputed by terms and concepts. Everything is labeled by a conceptual thought onto a certain basis of imputation. There is the label, there is that which labels things and then there is the basis upon which the label is given. So, phenomena exist as a result of all these things and the interaction between them. In his *Four Hundred Stanzas*, Aryadeva says, "If there is no imputation by thought, even desire and so forth have no existence. Then who with intelligence would maintain that a real object is produced dependent on thought?" In the commentary, *Mind Training Like the Rays of the Sun*, we read, "Undoubtedly, those that exist only through the existence of thought and those that do not exist when there is no thought are to be understood as not existing by way of their own entities, just as a snake is imputed onto a coiled rope." The example I gave earlier is how perceiving snow as yellow is a distorted perception. The example of distorted perception given here is mistaking a coiled rope for a snake.

Several conditions and factors need to come together for a person to misapprehend a coiled rope as a snake. It's not enough just to have a coiled rope in a corner on a bright day. No one is going to be fooled by that. There has to be some obscuration or darkness and distorted perception in the mind as well. Only then can the misapprehension take place. Even if we analyze every inch of that coiled rope we will not find a snake. In the same way, even if we analyze every aspect of self or phenomena we will not find inherent existence.

In the mind training text we find the following explanation. "An easier way of reaching a conviction about the way the innate misconception of self within our mind-stream gives rise to the misconception of self of persons and phenomena is that, as explained before, when a rope is mistaken for a snake, both the snake and the appearance of a snake in relation to the basis are merely projected by the force of a mistaken mind. Besides this, from the point of view of the rope, there is not the slightest trace of the existence of such an object [as a snake], which is merely projected by the mind. Similarly, when a face appears to be inside a mirror, even a canny old man knows that the appearance in the mirror of the eyes, nose and so forth and the reflection is merely a projection. Taking these as examples it is easy to discern, easy to understand and easy to realize that there is not the slightest trace of existence from the side of the object itself." The moment that a person thinks that there is a snake where the coiled rope lies, the appearance of a snake arises in that person's mind. That appearance, however, is nothing but a projection.

Similarly, although there isn't a self that exists independently and objectively, our grasping misapprehends the self to exist in that way. So then how does the self exist? Like any other phenomenon, the self exists imputedly. It exists by labeling, or imputation, by terms and concepts projected onto a valid basis of imputation. We must be able to clearly distinguish between the imputed self that is the basis for performing karmic actions and experiencing their results, and the inherently existent self that is the object that needs to be negated. When we consider our own sense of self, we don't really get the sense of an imputed self. The feeling we have is more as if the self were existing inherently. Let me explain how the labeling, or imputation, works.

People use names for one another but those names aren't the person. The words "John" and "Francis" are merely labels for a person. Just as the reflection of a face in a mirror does not exist from the side of the face, in the same way, the names John and Francis don't exist independently. The names are applied to a valid basis of imputation—that is, the person. When you apply a label onto any base of any phenomenon, it works to define that thing's existence—a vase, a pillar, a shoe and so forth. They are merely labels applied to their respective valid bases of imputation.

There is a common conceptual process involved in labeling things. Things don't exist from their own side, but they are labeled from our subjective point of view and that's how they exist. Let's take the example of a vase that we used earlier. In order to understand the selflessness, or emptiness, of the vase, we need to refute its inherent, true or independent existence, just as we have to refute the inherent, or true, existence of a person in order to understand the selflessness of a person. We must also be able to establish what a vase is conventionally or nominally because we cannot annihilate the conventional reality of a vase.

Conventionally, a vase exists. It is made out of whatever materials were used to create it. It has hundreds and thousands of atoms and then there is its design, the influence of the potter and so forth. All these factors contribute to the production of a vase. So, a vase exists as a mere labeling, or imputation, onto the various factors that form its conventional existence, that is, its valid basis of imputation. If we look for what is being imputed, if we look for "vase," we cannot find it. Just as we cannot find the imputed vase through ultimate analysis, we cannot find the imputed person through ultimate analysis.

The person, self or I is neither the continuity nor the continuum of a person, nor his or her collection or assembly of aggregates. So, what is a person? Chandrakirti gives the example of how the existence of a chariot depends upon the collection of its various parts. In today's terms we could use the example of a car. When we examine a car we discover that no single part is "car." The front wheels are not the car, the back wheels are not the car, neither is the steering wheel or any other part of it; there is no car that is not dependent upon these individual parts. Therefore, a car is nothing but a mere imputation onto its assembled parts, which constitutes its valid basis of imputation. Once the various parts of a car have been put together, the term "car" is imputed onto it. Just as a car is dependent upon its parts, so too is everything else.

Chandrakirti continues, "In the same way, we speak of a sentient being conventionally, in dependence upon its aggregates." So, we should understand that a person also depends upon his or her collection of aggregates. No one aggregate is the person, self, or I, yet there isn't a person who is not dependent upon their aggregates. A person or sentient being is nothing but a label projected onto his or her valid basis. As we find stated in the mind training text, "Such a technique for determining the selflessness of the person is one of the best methods for cognizing the reality of things quickly. The same reasoning should be applied to all phenomena, from form up to omniscient mind."

REFUTING INHERENT EXISTENCE THROUGH VALID REASONING

We need to use our intelligence to establish that the way in which our innate ignorance perceives the self to exist is not really the way that the self exists at all. This is what we call "refuting inherent existence through valid reasoning." It is not enough to say, "Everything is emptiness" or "Things don't inherently exist." We need a process of sound reasoning to back up this viewpoint. Once we have that, we will understand that there isn't anything that exists objectively. However, this is still only an intellectual understanding. We have to develop an intimacy between our perception and the true understanding of emptiness.

When we gain what is known as "definite ascertainment"—certitude with regard to the absence of inherent existence—we will be able to realize emptiness *experientially*. To substantiate this point, the mind training text offers a quote from the Indian master Dignaga's *Compendium of Valid Cognition*. "Without discarding this object, one is unable to eliminate it." This is telling us that once we have discovered the object of apprehension of our self-grasping—that is, the inherently existent self—we then need to train our mind to get rid of the idea of this object from our perception.

We must be aware of three examples of mistaken approaches to emptiness. The first example is of people who don't even allow their minds to investigate what self and selflessness are. They just never engage themselves in these questions. People with this kind of attitude will never be able to cultivate the wisdom realizing emptiness because they haven't made any kind of connection with the concept. Again we find a quote from Dignaga's *Compendium*: "Since love and so forth do not directly counter ignorance, they cannot eliminate that great fault." What this tells us is that even if we cultivate any or all of the four immeasurables—immeasurable love, immeasurable compassion, immeasurable joy and immeasurable equanimity—we still will not be able to understand selflessness. However wonderful these attitudes may be, they do not directly counteract the way in which our innate grasping perceives the self to exist.

The second example is given in another quote from the text: "We acquaint ourselves with a non-conceptual state in which thoughts about whether things are existent or non-existent, whether they are or are not, no longer arise." This refers to people who remain in a blank state of mind during their meditation, without investigating the nature of existence. They stop all kinds of conceptual thoughts. It's almost as if they are in a state of nothingness. Such people also will not understand selflessness, for they have exaggerated the object of refutation and refuted too much. They consider every conceptual thought as if it were the object of refutation; as if to allow a conceptual thought to enter one's mind would be to accept the inherent existence of that thought. They view all thought processes as something to be abandoned. Therefore, they don't think about anything at all. They have confused what is being refuted through valid reasoning—the inherent existence of the self, or I—with something that actually conventionally exists, that is, a thought. In other words, they have taken conventional existence as being identical with inherent existence.

If the wonderful attitudes of love, compassion, joy and equanimity cannot directly counteract our innate self-grasping, how can thinking about nothing achieve this aim? If we stop thinking about anything, that is not a meditation on emptiness because we are not allowing the wisdom understanding emptiness to arise. If we could ever reach the state of enlightenment by this method we would be buddhas without omniscient wisdom or compassion, because we would not have let anything arise in our minds. I encourage you to investigate this for yourselves.

The next example of this mistaken approach to emptiness is, "If, in meditation, following analysis of the general appearance of what is negated, our analytical understanding differs from the meaning intended or we meditate merely on a non-conceptual state in which we do not recognize emptiness, no matter how long we do this meditation, we will never be able to rid ourselves of the seed of the misconception of self." What this is saying is that if we refute inherent existence through valid reasoning and then meditate on something else, our meditation is not going to work. The text continues, "The third mistaken approach is to have established something other than the view of selflessness through analytical awareness so that when we meditate, our meditation is misplaced." We will never realize selflessness with this approach either, because we have disconnected the focus of our valid reasoning from the focus of our meditation. This is, as the text describes, "like being shown the racetrack but running in the opposite direction."

INTERPRETATIONS OF EMPTINESS BY EARLIER MASTERS

In order to realize what selflessness is, we have to understand the self that does not exist. Different schools of Buddhist thought have different interpretations in regard to this. The commentary on one of Lama Tsong Khapa's greatest works, *The Essence of Eloquent Presentation on that which is Definitive and that which is Interpretable*, tells us that Tsong Khapa asserted that many earlier Tibetan masters, although endowed with many great qualities, somehow missed the true meaning of emptiness. By "earlier Tibetan masters" Tsong Khapa is referring to the period after the eighth century when Acharya Padmasambhava and Abbot Sangharakshita were invited to Tibet and also to the period after the eleventh century, including the arrival of Atisha up until the time of Tsong Khapa in the fourteenth century. What Lama Tsong Khapa meant was that in terms of the aspect of the path, which has to do with method or skillful means, these masters had innumerable great qualities such as bodhicitta. They had perfected the method aspect of Buddhism, but somehow many of them had missed the view of emptiness. They couldn't quite grasp it completely. Then, in the eleventh century, the great Indian master Atisha was invited to Tibet. He composed a very beautiful text called *Lamp for the Path to Enlightenment*, and with this work Atisha refined the complete teachings of the Buddha, including both sutra and tantra.

In the fourteenth century, Lama Tsong Khapa realized the view of emptiness with the help of the deity, Manjushri. Tsong Khapa said that in order to understand emptiness, our understanding must be free from the two extremes of refuting too much and refuting too little. Some earlier Tibetan masters did not precisely identify the object of refutation. They asserted that the ultimate truth is findable under ultimate analysis. This is a case of underestimating the object of refutation. They have not refuted enough and, in so doing, have missed the view of emptiness. We need to purify much negativity and accumulate great merit in order to realize emptiness. If such great masters can miss it, we can easily miss it as well.

## EMPTINESS IN DIFFERENT BUDDHIST SCHOOLS

There are four essential points of Buddhism called the "four seals"— every composite phenomenon is impermanent; everything that is contaminated or deluded is suffering in nature; everything that exists is selfless, or empty; and nirvana, or liberation, is peace. All Buddhists accept these four points as definitive teachings, but in regard to the third point—that all phenomena are selfless, or empty—different Buddhist schools have different interpretations.

Theravadins interpret the third seal as meaning only that there is no self of a person. This Buddhist tradition does not accept the self-lessness of phenomena. Within the four major tenet schools of Buddhism—Vaibhashika, Sautrantika, Cittamatra and Madhyamaka—we find different assertions and presentations with regard to selflessness, and also in regard to the object of refutation. The two lower schools are the Vaibhashika—sometimes called Particularists or Realists—and the Sautrantika—Followers of Sutra. Like the higher schools, the tenets of these schools say that there isn't a self-sufficient and substantially existent self of a person. However, they also only assert the selflessness of a person and not the selflessness of phenomena.

As we go higher in Buddhist philosophy we find the Cittamatra, or Mind Only, school of thought. Their presentation is different. They talk about two types of selflessness, the selflessness of persons and the selflessness of phenomena. According to the Mind Only school, it is the "duality between subject and object" that is the object of negation or the thing that one is denying exists. They establish the selflessness of phenomena by saying that the subject and its object have the same nature and that it is the division between subject and object as being separate entities that is the object of negation. In other words, the subject and object are empty of being dual and separate entities.

The Mind Only school talks about three different categories of phe-nomena—"imputed phenomena," which do not exist by way of their own characteristics, and "thoroughly established phenomena" and "dependent phenomena," which do exist by way of their own characteristics.

As mentioned before, in the Middle Way school we find two sub-schools—the Prasangika-Madhyamaka and the Svatantrika-Madhyamaka. These two philosophical schools present selflessness differently. The Svatantrika-Madhyamaka school also talks about two kinds of selflessness, the selflessness of a person and the selfless-ness of phenomena. They agree with the Mind Only school that the selflessness of a person is easier to understand than the selflessness of the phenomenal world. They agree with the Mind Only School and the other two Buddhist schools as far as the selflessness of a person is concerned, but their selflessness of phenomena is different.

Most Buddhist schools assert that if something does not exist from its own side or by way of its own characteristics, it does not exist at all. The Svatantrika-Madhyamikas, however, assert that things do exist by way of their own characteristics but do not exist *truly*. So, according to this school, the terms "true existence" and "existing by way of its own characteristics" are not synonymous. The Svatantrika-Madhyamaka school asserts that everything exists as a *combination* of projection and inherent existence. They believe that things exist part-ly as a result of our mind's conceptual projections, or imputations, and partly from their own side. They believe that nothing exists in and of itself without labeling, or conceptual imputation, and this assertion is their object of negation, but they believe that things do exist from their own side to some degree. In other words, phenomena possess a characteristic that we can call objective existence.

In the highest Buddhist school of thought, the Prasangikas, it is said that nothing exists from its own side, even to the slightest extent. Everything is imputed, or labeled. Unlike other schools, they assert that the selflessness of a person does not simply mean that there is no self-sufficient or substantially-existent person. They talk about a per-son not existing inherently, or in and of itself. According to the

Prasangikas, the "emptiness of true existence" and the "emptiness of inherent existence" mean the same thing. Like the Mind Only and Svatantrika-Madhyamaka schools, the Prasangikas assert two types of selflessness, the selflessness of a person and the selflessness of phenomena. However, in terms of what is being refuted, they assert that there isn't any difference between them. One is just as easy to understand as the other because the process of discovering them is the same. Supposing that you as the meditator want to focus on the selflessness of I, using the person as the basis. When, through reasoning, you perceive the selflessness of I, as you shift your focus onto any other object or phenomenon you can understand the selflessness of that phenomenon by the power of the same reasoning. You don't need to re-establish the selflessness of phenomena using some other method.

For the Prasangika school, there is not even a subtle difference between the selflessness of a person and the selflessness of phenomena. When we realize that a person exists through mere labeling by terms and concepts and does not exist in and of itself we have realized the selflessness of a person. Taking phenomena as our focus, when we realize phenomena as mere labeling by terms and concepts and not existing in and of themselves, we have realized the selflessness of phenomena. There is a difference with regard to the basis of imputation, but there isn't any difference between the two types of selflessness in terms of what they actually are. It is for that reason that Chandrakirti states that "selflessness is taught in order for sentient beings to be liberated from cyclic existence. The two kinds of selflessness are simply posited on their bases of imputation." When we take a person as the basis of imputation, we are dealing with the selflessness of a person. When we take any other phenomenon as the basis of imputation, we are dealing with the selflessness of phenomena.

According to the Svatantrika-Madhyamikas and the three schools below them, phenomena are not just names or labels. They assert that phenomena should be findable under what is known as "ultimate analysis." When things are found under this type of analysis, they say we can validate the existence of these phenomena. When something is not findable under this kind of analysis, they are not able to assert its existence.

The assertion of the Prasangika-Madhyamaka school is totally different. According to the Prasangikas, *nothing* should be findable under ultimate analysis. If something is found then that thing must truly exist, and it is true existence, or findability under ultimate analysis, that is the object of refutation according to this school. Arya Nagarjuna said, "Knowing that all phenomena are empty like this and relying on actions and their results is a miracle amongst miracles, magnificence amidst magnificence." So, even though we understand the emptiness of all phenomena, we still rely upon the understanding of the infallible nature of cause and effect.

According to the Prasangika-Madhyamaka school, the terms "existing by way of its own characteristic," "inherent existence" and "true existence" all mean the same thing. For the Prasangikas, all these terms describe the object of negation—the kind of existence that is being refuted or negated. For that reason, our innate grasping at the inherent existence of the self (that is, the innate grasping at the self, existing by way of its own characteristics) is a distorted perception. It is exactly that distorted perception that needs to be cut through and eliminated by cultivating the wisdom that understands emptiness.

THE MEANING OF I, OR SELF, IN DIFFERENT BUDDHIST SCHOOLS

All Buddhist schools of thought agree that the I, or self, constitutes the focus of our innate grasping. Where they differ, however, is in terms of what a person is. Certain lower Buddhist schools assert that a person is their five physical and mental aggregates. Other schools say that it's just the mind that is the person and not the other aggregates. In the Mind Only school there is one sub-school that follows a sutra tradition and another that follows reasoning. The sutra followers of the Mind Only school assert that the mind is the person.

The majority of Buddhist schools assert six consciousnesses—the five sensory consciousnesses (eye consciousness, ear consciousness, nose consciousness, tongue consciousness and body consciousness) and mental consciousness. In addition to these six consciousnesses, however, the sutra followers of the Mind Only school talk about "deluded mental consciousness" and "mind basis of all," sometimes translated as "store consciousness." According to them, the mind basis of all is the person and as such it is the focus of the deluded mental consciousness. Those who assert this position say that all our karmic actions deposit their imprints on this particular consciousness.

According to Bhavaviveka, the great Indian master of the Svatantrika-Madhyamaka school, the person is a stream of mental consciousness. So, according to these two schools, when we create karmic actions, the imprints of these actions are stored or deposited on this mind-stream. The reason that the sensory consciousnesses don't store any of these imprints is because they only function here and now. When we die they cease to exist. They are confined to this existence and so cannot become connected to our future lives. Bhavaviveka has presented his position or assertion of what a person is in his work called *Blaze of Reasoning*.

Now, all the Buddhist schools of thought agree that the person, or self, is an imputed phenomenon—something that is imputed onto its aggregates. Yet, when you ask many of them to pinpoint what that imputed self is, the examples they give are some kind of substantially existent self, or person. Such is the case with some of the assertions we have just been considering. According to the Buddhist school of thought below the Svatantrika-Madhyamaka school, in order to know whether something exists, its existence must be proved by a valid cognition. According to these schools, when we look for a phenomenon it should be findable under analysis. When you find something under such analysis, that thing is said to exist by way of its own characteristics. If you don't find something, then that means that thing doesn't exist at all. However, according to the Prasangika-Madhyamaka school, things should not be findable under ultimate analysis. If you find something, you've gone wrong. That is how the Prasangika position totally opposes that of these other schools.

According to the Prasangika-Madhyamaka school, when you investigate self, you will not find anything such as a person existing from its own side at the end of your analysis. A person is merely a projection that is imputed onto the aggregates. If you do find a person existing from its own side, it should be inherently existent, existing in and of itself, which is impossible because things exist dependently.

## THE DIFFICULTY OF UNDERSTANDING EMPTINESS

These are very technical points and you need to take time to think about them. After contemplating the profundity of these teachings, you may simply come to the conclusion that the wisdom realizing emptiness is too difficult to achieve. It is important to understand that however difficult it is, with perseverance and the passage of time, you *will* be able to see progress within yourself and gain this wisdom. This is simply the law of nature. If we keep doing something, through the power of familiarization, it gradually becomes easier to do.

You may find it very hard even to conceptualize the view of emptiness, especially at the beginning, but think positively and make continuous effort. If you keep inspiring yourself, you can develop what is called an "affinity" with the view of emptiness—an inkling of what it all means, even if you don't yet have a full understanding. You develop a positive doubt about the nature of reality, a question as to whether things actually exist in the way that they normally appear to you. Such positive doubt is somewhat in tune with what we might call the "music" of emptiness and is said to be very beneficial and powerful. The text states that, "Buddha, the transcendent subduer, prophesied that the protector, Nagarjuna, would establish the unmistaken, definitive and interpretable meaning of emptiness as the essence of his teaching." The commentary given on these lines explains that before he spoke on emptiness Buddha knew that ordinary people would find it difficult to understand these concepts. So, even though you may find it very difficult to follow this teaching, you must never give up hope. Determine that you are going to make every effort to understand and please remember that it is better to put your effort into these matters by trying to understand them slowly. After all, if you don't want to suffer any more, you have no choice!

## DEFINITIVE AND INTERPRETABLE TEACHINGS

All the teachings of the historical Buddha are contained in the sutras and can be classified into two groups—definitive teachings, which need no elucidation, and interpretable teachings, which require explanation. A definitive teaching is one that can be accepted literally, in the way that Buddha presented it. An interpretable teaching is one that, if it were accepted as it is literally presented, would cause misunderstanding. The Buddha predicted the coming of two great spiritual pioneers, Arya Nagarjuna and Arya Asanga, who would illustrate the real meaning of his teachings and distinguish both their definitive and interpretable nature.

There is a sutra passage that states, "Father and mother are to be killed. The subjects and the country are to be destroyed. Thereby you will attain the state of purity." This passage is obviously an example of Buddha's interpretable teaching, as it requires interpretation.

The background to this passage is something that took place in the ancient Indian city of Rajgir, in the present state of Bihar. Devadatta, a cousin of the Buddha who was always trying to compete with him, befriended a young prince named Ajatashatru. Devadatta poisoned the prince's ears, saying that his father the king was clinging to the throne. He plotted with the prince to have the king assassinated so that Ajatashatru could take his place. Devadatta also plotted to kill the Buddha because he was jealous of Buddha's spiritual attainments. Devadatta told the prince, "I have a beautiful plan. Your father often invites the Buddha and his followers for alms, so you should ask the Buddha and his entourage to lunch. Dig a big fire pit right before the entrance to your palace and cover it so that it's well hidden. Buddha always walks ahead of his monks so, when he steps onto the pit, he will fall in and burn to death." The prince argued that the Buddha was too clever to be deceived, but Devadatta told him that, to be certain, he should poison Buddha's food in case the first plan didn't succeed.

One day, when the king was not at home, the young prince invited Buddha and his monks to the palace for lunch. He constructed a fire pit and poisoned the food just as Devadatta had instructed him. However, when Buddha placed his foot on the hidden fire pit, it instantly turned into a beautiful lake covered with lotus flowers. Buddha and the entire sangha walked safely across the lake on these flowers and entered the palace. The young prince was totally amazed and immediately confessed to Buddha that he wouldn't be able to serve the lunch because it was poisoned. Buddha told him to go ahead and bring the food anyway. When his meal arrived the Buddha blessed it and ate it without any harm coming to him. Meanwhile, the assassins who had been sent by the prince had caught his father. Before they killed him, the king asked them to take a message back to his son. The message read, "By killing me you have committed two heinous crimes of boundless negative karma because I am your father and an arhat, having already achieved the state of freedom." When Ajatashatru received this message he felt tremendous remorse for his actions. The emotional burden was so great that he felt he would die right then and there. He decided to go to the Buddha and tell him everything. Buddha wanted to give the prince more time to do confession and purification and so he told him, "Father and mother are to be killed and if you destroy the king and his ministers and subjects, you will become a pure and perfect human being."

Of course, at that moment the prince didn't understand the meaning behind the Buddha's statement, but later on when he had given it more thought he realized that the terms "father" and "mother" stood for contaminated karmic actions and delusions and that these were to be killed, or destroyed, within himself. The remainder of the passage meant that other negativities associated with negative karmic actions and delusions also needed to be destroyed in the sense of being purified, and by doing that the prince would be able to attain the state of pure and perfect liberation.

The *Heart Sutra* is another example of an interpretable sutra, because it contains many statements that require explanation. For example, it doesn't make any sense to say "no ear, no nose, no tongue," and so forth. We know all these things exist. We need to understand that what Buddha really meant by these terms is that the ear, nose and tongue don't exist *inherently*.

An example of Buddha's definitive teaching is the sutra that presents the "four seals" of Buddhism. As I mentioned before, the four seals are that every composite phenomenon is impermanent, that which is contaminated is suffering in nature, everything that exists is empty, or selfless, and nirvana is peace. This teaching doesn't require any additional interpretation.

When we don't know how to differentiate between the definitive and interpretive teachings of Buddha, we get really confused. The Tibetans say that we make porridge of our misunderstanding. There is a very popular statement from the sutras: "O bhikshus and wise men, you should analyze and investigate my teaching just as a goldsmith analyzes gold. Just as a goldsmith tests gold by cutting it, rubbing it and burning it, so should you examine and investigate my teaching. Do not accept my teaching just out of devotion to me." So, just as a goldsmith tests gold in three ways, so should we examine and analyze the validity of Buddha's teaching through what are known as the "three types of valid cognition."

First, there is "direct valid perception." Then there is "inferential valid perception," which is not direct but based on reasoning. Finally, we use another form of inferential valid perception, which is more like a form of conviction based upon authentic reasoning. Having applied these three kinds of investigation, when we discover the refined gold-like teaching of Buddha, we should then adopt and practice it.

Buddha taught different things to different people at different times and under different circumstances. So, one thing we must do is understand the context of the situation in which he gave the teaching and to whom it was addressed. Without taking all these factors into consideration we cannot understand Buddha's intention. This is why it is important to study both the definitive and the interpretable teachings.

Another reason we talk about the three types of valid cognition, or perception, is that we find three different types of phenomena in the world. There are manifest objects, or obvious phenomena—those we can directly perceive with our senses. Then there are other kinds of phenomena that are hidden or concealed—we cannot perceive them directly and so we need to use inference in order to understand them. These phenomena need to be realized through valid reasoning and that is why we talk about inferential valid cognition. Third, within these concealed phenomena, there are those that are even more subtle and obscured. In order to perceive these, we need to rely upon authoritative or what are called "valid statements" by an unmistaken enlightened being. This is how we develop the conviction to perceive more obscured phenomena. For example, the text mentions that the great

Indian master Atisha follows the elucidation of Arya Nagarjuna in terms of presenting emptiness. Therefore, Atisha's presentation of emptiness is authoritative and valid and the author advises us that we can feel confident in following it.

FOUR

# LEARNING TO BECOME A BUDDHA

## PERFECT ABANDONMENT AND PERFECT REALIZATION

To become a completely enlightened person, a buddha, we must fulfill two levels of achievement—the "level of perfect abandonment" and "the level of perfect realization." In order to achieve perfect realization we need to travel the structured spiritual path. We begin by cultivating great compassion. When great compassion arises in our mind, the Mahayana seed has been activated within us. We are then able to generate the altruistic mind of enlightenment, or bodhicitta, which we can also call the bodhisattva spirit. As we progress through the five spiritual paths—the path of accumulation, the path of preparation, the path of seeing, or insight, the path of meditation and the path of no more learning—we also progress through what are known as the "ten spiritual grounds of bodhisattvas." When we complete the five paths and ten grounds, we reach the state of highest enlightenment. We keep on discarding what are known as the "objects of abandonment" along the way—the things we must get rid of in order to progress—and we continue accumulating realizations. Eventually, we will have what is known as "omniscient wisdom," the all-knowing wisdom of a buddha. That is the perfect realization.

Perfect abandonment is something we can accomplish by way of eliminating the two major mental obscurations—the obscurations to personal liberation and the obscurations to the omniscient state. We should slowly try to purify the negativities we have already accumulated and try not to create new ones. We are not able to remember our past lives but we should try to understand the existence of former lives through inference from our present one. In this life, we do not find it difficult to do the wrong things. It seems so natural and easy to engage in negativities that it's as if we are magnetically drawn to them. From this we can infer that in many previous lifetimes we created and accumulated tremendous negativities that we need to purify.

If we just keep on repeating negative actions without purifying them, after some time we might lose all hope and think that nothing can save us. It all feels too much. It seems impossible to purify our negativities and to stop creating more because it has become a way of life. Let's say we have taken out a loan. If we don't pay back anything, the interest keeps on accumulating and after some time the debt becomes totally unmanageable. The wise thing to do is to pay the loan back slowly in small installments. If we do this, then one day we will have paid back all the money we borrowed and we won't need to worry any more.

In the same way, we need to purify our old debt-like negativities and not acquire new loan-like negativities. If we don't do that, but let them go on piling up, they become so powerful, so intense and captivating, that we may lose faith in our ability to purify them. These negativities then precipitate our rebirth in any one of the three unfortunate states, where we remain for eons. It is better not to fall into that kind of state in the first place. Strive instead for perfect abandonment and perfect realization.

## INTEGRATING BODHICITTA AND THE WISDOM OF EMPTINESS

If your goal is *just* to be liberated from cyclic existence, then the wisdom that perceives emptiness is the essential realization because that is the liberating path. If you don't have that wisdom, this cycle of compulsive rebirths will keep on spinning like a wheel and you will just keep wandering around within it. However, in order to follow the complete path that can lead to perfect abandonment and perfect realization, you have to integrate bodhicitta with the wisdom of emptiness. Bodhicitta is even more essential than the wisdom of emptiness for reaching buddhahood. Cultivating the wisdom that realizes emptiness is certainly wonderful and powerful, but if that kind of wisdom is not integrated with the altruistic mind of enlightenment, you won't be able to fulfill the two types of collection—the collection of merit and the collection of wisdom—or to attain the two enlightened bodies—rupakaya and dharmakaya.

You must learn how to cultivate bodhicitta, the bodhisattva's attitude, and you must follow and meditate on this way. It is not enough just to pray and hope that you may some day be able to experience bodhicitta. Nor is it enough to simply recite mantras and do your daily prayers. Of course, by doing prayers, reciting mantras and making such aspirational wishes, you are no doubt creating positive energy or merit, but if you don't cultivate the techniques for actually generating bodhicitta, you will never ever experience it. If you don't have the experience of bodhicitta, you must make every effort to cultivate it, and those of you who do shouldn't just stop there—you must make every effort to enhance this mind of enlightenment further.

At the same time, you must remember that the wisdom realizing emptiness is the only antidote to all your delusions, and without getting rid of your delusions, enlightenment is just a daydream. Again, simply making prayers, reciting mantras and sitting in a beautiful posture is not going to do the job. Until you achieve the paths of the transcendental beings—the path of seeing and beyond—you cannot stop creating new karmic actions that precipitate your rebirth in cyclic existence. When you have gained direct experience and realization into emptiness, you will be able to see the law of karmic action and result as if it were functioning right under your nose.

Someone with excellent eyesight is not going to make the mistake of falling off a cliff. Likewise, when you have direct experience of and realization into emptiness, you will no longer create any new negative karmic actions that send you over the cliff's edge into bad rebirths. This is not something that you should just keep at the back of your mind. It is something that you must clearly understand and in which you must develop confidence.

In an abbreviated version of the *Wisdom Gone Beyond*, or the *Perfection of Wisdom*, we find that of the six perfections, it is the perfection of wisdom that liberates us from our delusions. If the perfection of wisdom is eliminated, the remaining five can no longer be called perfections. The other perfections of giving, ethics, enthusiastic perseverance, patience and concentration are like auxiliary practices that enable us to develop this wisdom. The perfection of wisdom is likened to someone with perfect eyesight, while the other five are compared to five blind friends. The perfection of wisdom is the guide that can lead the others to their destination.

## PREPARING TO MEDITATE ON EMPTINESS

The wisdom realizing emptiness as the final mode of existence ultimately arises through meditation practice, so we need to learn the techniques of meditation. When we enter this spiritual path, it is not enough just to study and listen to teachings. It is more important to do our practices. This also includes the practice of purification and the practice of the two accumulations of merit and wisdom. To be able to meditate on emptiness, we must first study or listen to teachings on the subject. Another important part of the process is to cultivate the causes and conditions that will prepare us to be suitable practitioners of emptiness. We have already reviewed the preliminaries that are covered in *Mind Training Like the Rays of the Sun*. In particular, there are four preliminaries that we must understand and cultivate before proceeding with our study and meditation on emptiness.

- We should contemplate the preciousness of our human life, which is characterized by all kinds of freedoms and enriching factors.
- We need to contemplate the inevitability of our own death and the impermanence of all phenomena.
- We have to study the infallible law of karmic actions and their results.
- Based upon all these contemplations, we should cultivate the determined wish to be liberated from the repetitive cycles of existence.

Of these preliminaries, perhaps the most important is cultivating the determined wish to be liberated from cyclic existence. Having studied and practiced these to a certain extent, we should then focus on the practice of emptiness. We always need to reconnect to our spiritual goal; remember that the reason we are studying and trying to engage in spiritual practice is because we want to become buddhas for the sake of all other sentient beings. As we have seen, even if we have the wonderful attitudes of immeasurable love, immeasurable compassion, immeasurable equanimity and immeasurable joy, without the wisdom realizing emptiness, we cannot eliminate our root ignorance. Only this wisdom can cut through our innate self-grasping. Some people may think, "Maybe if I go for some profound tantric empowerments, that will do the magic for me." However, simply attending and receiving initiations is not going to do the job either. When we take empowerments we commit ourselves to certain practices and vows that we are required to keep. If we break these commitments, we will take a bad rebirth. Therefore, if we are unprepared, receiving empowerments can become an obstacle instead of a benefit.

Let's say there is a source of water but the amount of water is far greater than you need and you lay a pipeline to drain off enough for yourself. Keeping the commitments of empowerments or initiations is as important as keeping that pipeline intact. If any cracks, holes or blockages appear in the pipe—in other words, if you break your commitments—you may think that you have maintained the connection to the source, but you are not going to receive any benefits or blessings from it. These will all seep out of the cracks and holes or simply not get through at all. Although it is good to receive tantric empowerments, keeping the accompanying commitments is much more important.

OBSTACLES TO MEDITATION—LAXITY AND EXCITEMENT

There are two major obstacles to meditation—laxity, or mental dullness, and excitement, or distraction. It is very important to learn to recognize laxity and excitement in both their coarse and subtle forms. If you don't, you can end up doing the wrong kind of meditation. Many Buddhist meditators have failed to recognize subtle laxity as an obstacle and have thought their meditation to be very advanced, thus wasting a lot of time. In his lam-rim text, the *Great Exposition of the Stages of the Path to Enlightenment,* Lama Tsong Khapa emphasizes the importance of recognizing precisely what the subtle forms of both laxity and dullness are.

Our mind should have clarity as well as a good grip on the object of meditation. If we don't have clarity, coarse laxity sets in. Sometimes we may have good clarity but our grip, our mental hold, on the object of meditation is loose. This means that our problem is subtle laxity. Laxity can be caused by many things, and as we identify these causes we can make the necessary adjustments to deal with them. For example, we experience coarse laxity if we eat too much food. The result is that we feel heavy and start to fall asleep. Eating at improper times or eating foods that are too rich can also cause laxity, as can depression or disappointment.

At such times we need to inspire ourselves not to get stuck in this state. One of the ways to do this is by remembering the pre-eminent qualities of the enlightened beings and how much effort they have made to become what they are and to help us, who are still trapped within samsara. In this way, we are reminded how much harder we need to work in our practices. Another way of dealing with laxity or mental sleepiness is to try to bring what we call the "brilliance of light" into our mind—to switch on the internal light of illumination. If that doesn't work, we should go and wash our face or take a walk. In short, to deal with laxity we should refresh ourselves.

Excitement or distraction happens when our mind is not really staying on the object of meditation. When we are sitting on our meditation cushion, we may begin to think about many things, either good or bad. There is a mental agitation that churns out all kinds of thoughts and ideas, such as all the things we have to do that day. When we do a good meditation we notice pins and needles in our feet and pain in our knees, but when we are distracted for the whole session, we don't feel any pain at all. When our mind wanders in this way, ego, pride and arrogance emerge and become a cause of excitement. Our minds become totally distracted and we are no longer meditating. We may begin to think about how other people see us or about our own personal history. We should not let such discursive thoughts enter our mind. We should not think about our profession or family matters, or about food, drink or gossip. It is better to think about these things before we start our meditation and take care of them then. If any such thoughts arise during meditation, we should stop them then and there and not allow them to function in our mind.

## Meditating on emptiness

In his concluding verse of a stanza in the *Three Principal Paths*, Lama Tsong Khapa writes, "Just like that, when you have understood and realized the vital points of the three principal paths, you should seek solitude, generate your power of enthusiasm and strive for the ultimate goal." The three principal paths are:

- The determined wish to be liberated, sometimes simply described as "renunciation."
- Bodhicitta, the altruistic mind of enlightenment.
- The wisdom perceiving emptiness.

We must study these points, contemplate the teachings on them and then cultivate them through meditation. It takes time to gain spiritual realizations. When you study or listen to the teachings you don't get experience. You can only get experience through meditation. Without meditation you can never experience the wisdom of emptiness, and without this wisdom you can never counteract your delusions.

The whole purpose of meditation is to achieve stability of mind, to enhance its potential and to gain freedom from difficulties and unwanted problems. Basically, there are two types of meditation—single-pointed, or stabilizing, meditation and analytical, or insight, meditation. Meditation means familiarizing our mind with whatever the object of meditation is. In order to practice meditation we must have an object to focus on. As we focus on this object, we try to keep our mind unperturbed and undistracted. In this way, we cultivate some intimacy and familiarity with the object of meditation. As I mentioned earlier, you can't simply sit keeping your mind free from all thought and imagine you are meditating. You are never going to achieve anything out of a blank mind.

Calm abiding, or single-pointed meditation, is where you simply try to set your mind on a chosen object. You can use anything you like as your focus and you then try to concentrate on that object without getting distracted by anything else. Calm abiding (*shamatha*) meditation is a very stabilized state of mind. In itself, it is not a really great achievement. You might attain some higher level of consciousness or develop some psychic abilities through calm abiding, but that's about it. In Buddhist practice, we don't feel complacent when we have calm abiding but use it more like a vehicle in which we can ride to the state of enlightenment. Our purpose for cultivating single-pointed concentration is not just to have a calm mind, but to use this mental stability to be able to practice much higher things and ultimately reach the state of enlightenment.

Calm abiding alone cannot counteract our afflictive emotions, our deluded states mind. We have attained calm abiding many times in previous lives. In this present life, we should try to use it in a more meaningful way—to deeply penetrate the ultimate nature of reality, the way in which everything actually exists. With this stable mind, we use analytical meditation to cultivate insight into and realization of emptiness. Calm abiding is very helpful for this, because our mind is so stable and firm that it can really focus on emptiness without distraction. Lama Tsong Khapa states that "riding on the horse-like calm abiding and using the sharp weapon of the middle way, you can cut through the net of distorted perceptions and grasping."

This example comes from ancient times when warriors would ride into battle on horseback. They had to have a good horse, sharp weapons and a strong, healthy body. Thus equipped, they could win battles. Putting this into a spiritual context, we need to ride on the good horse of calm abiding; if you're riding a bad horse, it will throw you off. The sharp, sword-like wisdom realizing emptiness is the real weapon we need. As well, we have to maintain the healthy body of pure discipline, or ethics. With these qualities we can overcome our actual enemy—the delusions within ourselves.

In the text, we find three major outlines dealing with selflessness and illusory perception. First we have to establish the view of the self-lessness of a person. Then we have to establish the selflessness of phenomena. Once we have directly perceived both types of selflessness in meditation, when we come out of the meditative state we can see all persons and everything else that exists as illusions.

With respect to emptiness, we should practice analytical meditation more than calm abiding, especially at the beginning. We need to establish what emptiness is—what it is that we're going to meditate upon—so we start with analytical meditation. We have to go through a process of reasoning in order to establish what emptiness of inherent, or true, existence actually is. We do this by developing an understanding of dependent arising. We then use this understanding to establish what emptiness is. We then fix our mind on emptiness as our object of meditation and concentrate single-pointedly upon it. If we try to concentrate on emptiness without first understanding what it is, our meditation will not work.

We do meditation for a purpose, and we must try to bring that purpose to mind when we meditate. Some people think that meditation is simply a good way to relax from the everyday stresses of life. That is not what meditation is for. At the very least, our motivation should be to gain freedom from the pains and problems of samsara. If you want to have a higher kind of motivation, then based upon your own experience of not wanting pains and problems and wishing for peace and happiness, you should think about how all other sentient beings have the same wish. You should then practice meditation in order to liberate all sentient beings, yourself included, from all forms of suffering and bring lasting peace and happiness to all.

It doesn't matter what kind of meditation you are going to do, if your mind is excited and distracted, you must first try to bring it to a peaceful level. This is why we need calm abiding.

We all have to breathe. So, based upon the natural vehicle of breath, try to contain your mind and deal with its excitement. When you breathe out, remain aware of the exhalation of breath and when you breathe in, remain aware of the inhalation of breath. One exhalation and one inhalation constitute what is known as one round of breath; count from seven to twenty-one rounds to calm your mind.

Use your own natural rhythm. Don't exaggerate the process by breathing more heavily or strongly than normal. That would be artificial. When you breathe in and out, that gentle or natural breath should be through your nostrils not through your mouth. If you mess up in your counting, it means that your mind got distracted. If you try to do this focused meditation on your breath right after you return home from work, it might prove a little difficult, but you should be able to do it after taking a little rest. Through this kind of focused meditation on your natural process of breathing, you are basically trying to bring your mind back to whatever is your object of meditation. Once your mind is brought to a certain relaxed state, you can begin your actual meditation. Maybe you want to meditate on the impermanence of life, on death and dying or on the infallible workings of the law of karmic actions and results. Maybe you want to do guru yoga meditation, where you visualize your guru or teacher. The same preparation should be done for any other kind of meditation including meditation on bodhicitta or the perfect view of emptiness.

Many people have the notion that meditation is easy, that you just close your eyes, sit properly and put your hands in a certain gesture. Sitting like that is just a posture. It's not meditation. We must know how to meditate. The Indian master, Acharya Vasubandhu, in his *Treasury of Knowledge*, states that you should be abiding in ethical discipline and should have received teachings on the practice you are trying to do and contemplated their meaning. When you have really understand the practice, you are ready for meditation. It's a process. If you do it that way, you won't go wrong.

BETWEEN SESSIONS

The text states, "In between meditation sessions, be like a conjurer." How can we be like a conjurer? Our usual perception of things is that they appear to exist from their own side. They seem to have a kind of solidified and fixed nature. However, there is a disparity between the way phenomena appear to our perception and the way they actually exist. So, between sessions, we should try to understand that the way things appear to us as fixed and independently existent is like a magician's trick. We must also understand that we ourselves are the magician who created this trick, for it is our own faulty perception that sees things as existing independently. We should always try to see through this illusion, even as we interact with it.

Most people perceive all things as if they existed inherently and grasp at and cling to that perceived inherent existence. There are other people who perceive the appearance of inherent existence but don't grasp at it—things appear to them as if they existed in and of themselves, but they are aware that things don't really exist in that way. Then there are people who are free of both appearance *and* grasping. Not only do these people not grasp at things as if they existed independently but to them, things don't even *appear* to exist in that way. The difference between these kinds of people is illustrated in the following example.

In ancient India (and still today in some parts), there were magicians who created optical illusions to entertain people. Using only rocks and sticks, they could create beautiful magical illusions of horses and elephants. The spectators, whose visual perception was influenced by the magician's incantation, would actually see horses and elephants and believe them to be real. The spectators are like those people to whom phenomena appear as inherently existent and who also grasp at things as if they existed in that way. The magician himself would also see the horses and elephants, but the difference was that he knew the tricks he was playing; he knew he had created them. The magician is like those people to whom phenomena appear as inherently existent but who know that things don't actually exist that way. There would also be people whose consciousness had not been affected magical incantations—they wouldn't see any horses or elephants, so they wouldn't grasp at them. They are like people for whom there is neither the appearance of nor the grasping at the inherent existence of phenomena.

Ordinary people like us—ordinary in the sense that we have not realized what the ultimate nature of phenomena is—experience both the appearance of and the grasping at true and inherent existence. Things appear to us as if they exist truly, objectively and independently and we grasp at this perceived mode of existence because we think that things really do exist in this way. On the other hand, those who have gained direct insight into emptiness may also experience the appearance of inherent existence of phenomena, but they don't grasp at this appearance because they know the truth of how things actually exist. Then there are the *aryas*, transcendental beings who have directly and non-conceptually experienced what emptiness is. When they are in meditative equipoise on emptiness, neither does inherent existence of phenomena appear to them nor is there grasping at such existence.

The reason you keep going round and round in this compulsive cycle of rebirths is that you do not understand ultimate reality. When you engage in your practices, you shouldn't do so with the idea that maybe, in some mysterious way, your practice is going to make you enlightened in the far distant future or that perhaps it will help ward off some negative influence. You must do your practices for the purpose of cultivating bodhicitta and the wisdom realizing emptiness. When you make offerings, recite mantras or help the poor and needy, you should dedicate the merit of such actions to gaining these realizations. To really understand emptiness, you must meditate consistently over a number of years and continually do purification and accumulation practices. But don't let this dishearten you. Through constant effort and with the passage of time, you will definitely come to understand emptiness.

# Five

# Dedication

We need to properly dedicate the merit we have gained through studying this teaching. Let us dedicate our collective merit for the flourishing of Buddhadharma, the source of benefit and happiness for everyone throughout the universe, and for the long life of His Holiness the Dalai Lama and all the other great masters from any spiritual tradition. May they live long and be successful in fulfilling their visions and dreams for sentient beings.

May spiritual communities throughout the world and spiritual practitioners of all kinds remain healthy, happy and harmonious and be successful in fulfilling their spiritual aspirations. May this and other world systems be free from all kinds of unwanted pains and problems, such as sickness, famine and violence, and may beings experience peace, happiness, harmony and prosperity.

Last, but not least, let us dedicate our collective spiritual merit for all sentient beings to be free from the fears and dangers of the two types of mental obscuration and from all kinds of pains and problems and may we all quickly reach the state of highest enlightenment.

PART TWO

# A COMMENTARY
# ON
# *The Heart Sutra*

# ONE

# INTRODUCTION

## MOTIVATION

I personally feel extremely fortunate to have this opportunity to teach the *Heart Sutra*, otherwise known as the *Perfection of Wisdom* or the *Wisdom Gone Beyond*. I also feel that you, too, as participants in this teaching, are very fortunate.

Why should we feel fortunate to be able to participate in this teaching? Firstly, this human life is extremely precious and very hard to achieve. Secondly, it is very rare that a buddha, an enlightened being, manifests as an emanation body in our world. Lastly, it is very difficult to come into contact with the Mahayana, or Greater Vehicle, teaching of Buddhism. Even though it is only under exceptional circumstances that all these factors come together, somehow we have been able to achieve it. We have this wonderful life with all its freedoms and potential for liberation and we also have the opportunity to follow the Greater Vehicle teaching of the historical Buddha, Shakyamuni.

The *Heart Sutra* is special because by putting its teaching into practice it is possible for us to attain liberation from samsara, the cycle of existence, and to become enlightened within our own lifetime. Even though this is a short sutra, its meaning is extremely profound and we find a wealth of information within just a couple of pages. Take the time to reflect upon and contemplate the meaning. When we recite the *Heart Sutra*, we shouldn't rush our recitation as if skating on ice. Instead, we should try to understand what each word means and should not be afraid to ask those who know more than we do when our understanding fails us.

We will not gain much from the teachings if we listen with the sense of being coerced by some external force or authority. Only if we listen with our own inner spiritual enthusiasm can we listen fully. This enthusiasm flows from our understanding of the true value of the Dharma. When we ask, from the depths of our minds and hearts, what it is that we are truly seeking, then we can begin to realize the enormous value of spiritual practice in our present and future lives.

Remember that meditation practice is far more important than simply reading Dharma texts. We shouldn't spend too much time reading books, but should try to meditate as much as possible so that we can internalize and actualize the meaning of the teaching within our mind-stream. It is primarily through meditation that deep experiences and realizations come. A poor person doesn't gain much simply by knowing how much a rich person owns. In the same way, an intellectual understanding of emptiness does not benefit us much if we don't put it into practice and meditate on it.

Let us cultivate our altruistic intention, seeking enlightenment for the sake of liberating all sentient beings, who pervade limitless space. It is with this kind of motivation, the motivation of bodhicitta, that we should participate in this teaching.

## OUR BUDDHA NATURE

We have within us two types of buddha nature, or buddha lineage— our "naturally abiding buddha nature" and our "developable buddha nature." The naturally abiding buddha nature refers to the emptiness of our mind. As we engage in Dharma practice, we purify our negativities and accumulate wisdom and positive energy. It is through this practice that each of us can become a buddha. It is the emptiness of our infinite, all-knowing, or omniscient, mind that becomes the natural truth body of a buddha. This occurs when our mind is completely pure, free from defilements such as anger and pride and even of the imprints, or seeds, of those defilements.

Our developable buddha nature is the infinite potential of our mind to grow and develop spiritually through listening to, contemplating and meditating on the teachings. When our mind is completely free of the two obscurations—the obscurations to liberation (deluded emotions, such as anger and desire) and the obscurations to knowledge (ignorance born from dualistic perceptions)—it transforms into the all-knowing mind of a buddha.

## BACKGROUND TO *THE HEART SUTRA*

Shakyamuni Buddha was born in India over two thousand five hundred years ago. After generating bodhicitta—the altruistic mind of enlightenment—for three countless aeons, he then thoroughly perfected the two types of accumulation that constitute the fruition of the entire Mahayana path, the accumulations of merit, or positive energy, and wisdom, or insight. Eventually, he became an enlightened being—a fully awakened person.

Buddha performed twelve great deeds, but the most important deed of them all was turning the wheel of Dharma. Buddha gave the three great discourses that are known as the three turnings of the wheel of Dharma. The first wheel was turned in Sarnath and concerned the Four Noble Truths (*aryasatyas*). This teaching was primarily aimed at those who have the mental dispositions of the Hinayana, or Lesser Vehicle, practitioner. The third turning of the wheel was at Shravasti and concerned the characteristics of buddha nature.

It was on Vulture's Peak, a mountain near Rajgir in the present day state of Bihar, where Buddha turned the second wheel of Dharma. His discourse concerned the *Wisdom Gone Beyond* (*Prajnaparamita*) sutras, which include the *Heart Sutra*. Sutras and treatises deal with two types of subject matter—emptiness and the various levels of realization. The *Heart Sutra* explicitly presents emptiness as its subject matter and implicitly presents "the hidden levels of realization." The *Heart Sutra* is one of the most important of the Mahayana *Prajnaparamita* sutras. It is in the form of a dialogue between Shariputra, one of the Buddha's two closest disciples, and the bodhisattva Avalokiteshvara. The most extensive version of the *Prajnaparamita* sutras contains one hundred thousand verses; another contains twenty-five thousand verses, and there's also an abbreviated version eight thousand verses long. But the most concise version of the *Wisdom Gone Beyond* sutras is the *Heart Sutra*, which contains the innermost essence of them all.

## RECORDING THE SUTRAS

The sutras of Shakyamuni Buddha were not written down during his lifetime. However, when Buddha passed into *parinirvana*, final nirvana, there were many highly realized arhats and bodhisattvas who had great powers of mental retention, and they recorded everything the Buddha had taught about the *Wisdom Gone Beyond*.

Buddha passed into parinirvana, the state of solitary peace, during a spring full moon, on the fifteenth day of the fourth lunar month, according to the Tibetan calendar. It was later, during a summer retreat, that the great council was held, where as many as five hundred arhats assembled together to write down Buddha's teachings.

During the great council, the three master narrators of Buddha's works collected all of the teachings together. They are now found in the three divisions of the Buddhist canon, called the Three Baskets (*Tripitaka*). Mahakashyapa recalled all Buddha's teachings on higher knowledge (*abhidharma*). Then Upali narrated all the teachings given by Buddha on moral, or ethical, discipline (*vinaya*). Finally, Ananda, the Buddha's personal attendant, recalled and narrated all Buddha's teachings on the discourses (*sutras*).

When they had gathered for the great council, all the arhats folded their yellow robes (*chö-gö*) together and placed them one on top of the other to make a throne. The principal narrators sat on this throne of robes and recalled all the teachings given by Buddha. When it was Ananda's turn to sit upon the throne, he faced in the direction where Buddha had taught the *Prajnaparamita* and the other sutras. He remembered Buddha so deeply that he wept as he began to narrate the sutras. Thus, when you read the words at the beginning of sutras such as the *Heart Sutra*, in "Thus I have heard...," the "I" refers to Ananda.

## THE MEANING OF THE TITLE

In Sanskrit, the *Heart Sutra* is called *Bhagavati Prajnaparamita-hrdayam*. The Tibetans retained Sanskrit titles in their translations for two reasons. Firstly, it is believed the buddhas of the past, present and future give their teachings in Sanskrit, so by reading the title in Sanskrit, we plant the seeds of the source language of Dharma in our minds. The second reason is to help us remember the great kindness of the *lotsawas*, whose name comes from the Sanskrit term meaning, "eye of the world"—the great translators who originally translated this and other sutras from Sanskrit into Tibetan.

In order to understand the meaning of the Sanskrit title it is also helpful to know the Tibetan translation: *Chom-den-de-ma she-rab kyi pa-rol-tu chin-pay nying-po*. This line is actually an extremely concise statement of the doctrine of emptiness. It is regarded as the heart essence of the vast *Prajnaparamita* literature. *Chom-den-de-ma* relates to the word *bhagavati* in the title. *Chom* literally means "to destroy"; *den* means "to be in possession of remarkable qualities and realizations"; and *de* means "to go beyond." The Tibetan suffix *-ma* also relates to *bhagavati* and denotes that of the two aspects of Buddha's teaching, method (*upaya*) and wisdom (*jnana*), the *Heart Sutra* belongs to the mother-like, wisdom aspect.

The first part of the title signifies the state of nirvana beyond the two types of obscuration, which I mentioned before. *Prajna* means "wisdom" and *paramita* means "perfection" or "gone beyond." Thus *Bhagavati Prajnaparamita* can be translated as "the possession of the wisdom gone beyond." The Sanskrit word *hrdayam* relates to the Tibetan *nying-po*, which means "essence," translated here as "heart." So, the meaning of the title suggests that this sutra is the heart of all other *Wisdom Gone Beyond* sutras.

## THE WISDOM THAT PERCEIVES EMPTINESS

There are many kinds of wisdom but the *Wisdom Gone Beyond* sutra refers to the essential wisdom. This wisdom perceives the emptiness of true existence and thus the ultimate nature of all phenomena. It is with this wisdom that we can transcend ordinary levels of reality. Some other forms of wisdom include that arising from listening to teachings, the wisdom that arises from contemplating the teachings and the wisdom that arises from meditating on the teachings.

These wisdoms can themselves be divided even further, but they are all only complementary or auxiliary wisdoms to help us generate and cultivate the wisdom that perceives the emptiness of true existence. Buddha said that it is because sentient beings have not realized that emptiness is the true nature of phenomena that they wander in the various states of cyclic existence. It is our delusions, particularly our ignorance, that keep us here in samsara.

The root of all ignorance is our continual grasping at a self and it is this grasping that perpetuates our suffering. The wisdom that perceives emptiness is the direct antidote to this self-grasping and, as such, is essential in order for us to become liberated from the compulsive cycles of existence. Once we directly and nakedly realize the final and ultimate mode of existence of phenomena, we cease to create new causes to return to samsara.

The great Indian master, Aryadeva, in his treatise the *Four Hundred Stanzas*, clearly stated that even if one is not able to gain direct insight into the emptiness of all phenomena, merely by developing some positive doubt about the nature of reality, one can create a state of mind so powerful that it can shatter samsara. At the very least, if we think about and meditate on the meaning of emptiness every day, it will be of tremendous help in our spiritual growth. So, the *Wisdom Gone Beyond* refers to the wisdom that perceives emptiness, which itself is the very heart of wisdom.

INTRODUCTION TO EMPTINESS

This teaching focuses on the profound view of emptiness (*shunyata*), which we find in the *Wisdom Gone Beyond* sutras. This kind of teaching is meant for both those who have not yet realized the emptiness of true existence and those who have, to help them further their understanding. It is difficult to fully understand emptiness, but we must make every effort to do so. It is only through gaining this understanding and experience that we can liberate ourselves from the suffering of samsara, particularly the suffering of the three bad migrations, the unfortunate realms of rebirth.

If anyone thinks that by merely reciting a mantra they can liberate themselves from samsara, they are very mistaken. Likewise, simply cultivating great love, compassion and bodhicitta is not enough to completely remove delusion. Certainly, by reciting mantras and cultivating bodhicitta we can temporarily overcome manifest forms of delusion, but in order to eradicate delusion entirely, we must realize emptiness.

The way to generate an unmistakable understanding of emptiness in our own mind is by studying and listening to teachings on emptiness from qualified spiritual masters. However, the text states that emptiness is beyond words, expression or thought. How can we study something that is beyond words, expression or thought? What this statement means is that emptiness cannot be explained or even talked about without taking into consideration conventional phenomena as a basis or reference. There is no way to speak about emptiness directly, so we speak about it through its relation to certain phenomena.

Emptiness cannot be taught in the way that it exists for aryas in a state of meditative equipoise. Even they themselves cannot explain their experience to others. In the *Sutra of the Ten Spiritual Grounds of Bodhisattva Realization (Dashabhumisutra)*, it is written that when aryas watch a bird fly they can see and understand the trail that it leaves in the sky. Most people can see only the bird, but aryas can somehow see the path that the bird is following. Similarly, aryas can see the trail-like emptiness of all phenomena.

We cannot deal with emptiness in isolation. We have to talk about the basis upon which emptiness is established. For example, a wave is empty of true existence. When we focus our mind on the wave we see that the wave and the ocean cannot be differentiated. We see that they are dependent upon one another. The wave has no truly separate existence. In the same way, the experience of emptiness is non-dual, and in this state of non-duality our mind does not see the wave, only its emptiness. The wave then becomes the basis upon which emptiness as its ultimate characteristic is established.

Everything exists dependently upon everything else. Nothing exists independently in and of itself. Therefore, everything is empty of inherent existence. Every phenomenon is empty of true existence, therefore emptiness is the ultimate nature of everything that exists. Emptiness is a characteristic that all phenomena share. Like the wave, the self, or "I," is also a basis, and emptiness is its characteristic.

Emptiness is a very profound reality. We can understand this from the life story of the great master Lama Tsong Khapa, founder of the Gelug school of Buddhism. When he was in Central Tibet, he was deeply involved in intensive meditation. I mentioned before how once, while meditating on emptiness in the assembly of monks he was so absorbed that he didn't notice the other monks leave the assembly hall. I also explained how Lama Tsong Khapa reached such a high level of attainment that he was able to meet with the tantric deity of wisdom, Manjushri, and receive teachings directly from him.

Remember how Manjushri informed Lama Tsong Khapa that he had not yet fully realized emptiness and that in order to do so he needed to accumulate more positive energy, so Lama Tsong Khapa went into retreat at Wölka and practiced intensive purification and accumulation, doing innumerable prostrations and mandala offerings.

Realizing emptiness is no easy task. Even if we spend our entire life practicing meditation and reciting mantras, if we do not understand emptiness we cannot be liberated. We must realize that all the suffering we experience comes from the delusions in our minds. To cut through these delusions, we need the weapon of the wisdom that perceives emptiness.

Lama Tsong Khapa has stated that when we have made ourselves suitable recipients through cultivating the common paths or practices, we will be able to enter confidently into the tantric vehicle—the point of entry for the achievement of enlightenment. Before we receive a tantric empowerment, there are three conditions that are required of us. First, we must have the sincere wish to be liberated. Second, we must have generated the altruistic mind of enlightenment. And third, we must have the wisdom that perceives emptiness.

# Two

# The Meaning of the Text

## The Qualities of the Teacher

*"Thus I have heard. At one time the Lord was sitting on Vulture's Peak near the city of Rajgir."*

It was out of Buddha's own deep experiences and realizations and his infinite compassion for all sentient beings that he gave his teachings. Buddha is an incomparable master. His body, speech and mind are completely pure of defilements and even the imprints of defilements. His body, speech and mind are the result of completion and perfection in the process of the accumulation of excellence, that is, of positive energy and wisdom. It is our knowledge of Buddha's qualities and realizations that helps us develop unshakable faith, confidence and trust in him and his abilities.

The English translation of the text refers to the Buddha as "Lord." In the original Sanskrit this word is *bhagavan*, but it is more profound in the Tibetan translation, *chom-den-de*. As we mentioned earlier, the word *chom* literally means "to destroy." It is saying that Buddha has destroyed all defilements and the imprints of defilements. *Den* means "to possess excellent qualities and realizations"; *de* means to "go beyond" or "transcend." What this tells us is that in his enlightenment, Buddha has transcended the two extremes, which can refer to either the two types of obscurations or the two extremes of cyclic existence and solitary peace. This is why the Buddha is called *chom-den-de*. He is the destroyer of defilements, the possessor of excellent qualities and one who has gone beyond ordinary levels of reality.

The honorific term *bhagavan* is also used to refer to other holy people, so the translators added the word *de* to the original Sanskrit to indicate that this wasn't just an ordinary bhagavan but a truly transcendent one.

The city name of Rajgir literally means "the king's palace." This was where King Bimbisara, one of the Buddha's great royal patrons, lived. There are two interpretations given to the origin of the name of Vulture's Peak. Some people thought that the rock formations at the site looked like a flock of vultures. Others say that when Shakyamuni Buddha was teaching the *Prajnaparamita* sutras, the great bodhisattvas took the form of vultures when they came to receive the teaching.

## THE QUALITIES OF THE STUDENT

*"He was accompanied by a large community of monks as well as a large community of bodhisattvas."*

This tells us something about the excellent assembly, those who were witnesses to Buddha's teaching. This teaching was explicitly intended for bodhisattvas and those with bodhisattva inclinations, even though there were also shravakas (pious hearers) as well as ordinary monks among the gathering.

Emptiness cannot be taught to everyone, simply because not everyone has the capacity to understand it. As we find mentioned in the great Indian master Chandrakirti's work, *Supplement to the Middle Way*, a suitable recipient of the teaching of emptiness is someone who has already acquainted himself or herself with emptiness or teachings on emptiness and who is especially enthusiastic. There is an inner sign, an inner joy of the heart, which is sometimes expressed by tears rolling down the cheeks or by goose-bumps on the skin. Such a person has the right kind of mind to be able to comprehend the emptiness of true existence. Furthermore, based on their acquaintance with the subject of emptiness, such persons can grow spiritually to understand even deeper levels of realization.

The English translation of the text simply refers to a large community of monks and bodhisattvas. "Monk" is the common translation of the Sanskrit word *bhikshu*, but bhikshu can refer to people of varying levels of spiritual accomplishment. It can mean a person who has received full ordination, who relies upon the food that is given in alms and who enthusiastically engages in the practices of abandonment and meditation. There are also arya, or superior, bhikshus—those who have gained direct experience of emptiness. This third kind of bhikshu is one who is already in a state of liberation and has become an arhat—a full destroyer of delusion. The core disseminators of Buddha's teaching were this third kind of member of the community of bhikshus—bhikshus who had already attained this profound realization.

In the eight thousand verses of the *Wisdom Gone Beyond* sutra, we find that in the last community of monks before Buddha's death, all except one were arhats—completely free from contamination, defilement and delusion. The one exception was Ananda, the Buddha's personal attendant. Fortunately, Ananda achieved arhatship shortly before the great council was held.

The text states that the Buddha was also accompanied by "a large community of bodhisattvas." The Tibetan translation of the Sanskrit word bodhisattva is *jang-chub sem-pa.*" *Jang* literally means "pure of faults and defilements." *Chub* means "internally realized." *Sem-pa* is Tibetan for *sattva. Sem* means "to think" and *pa* means "to be brave." Taken together, the term literally translates to "hero." So a bodhisattva is a pure, realized person who thinks about the welfare of others and who works courageously towards the attainment of enlightenment for the sake of all, bravely cutting through the forces of negative actions.

Another interpretation of the word *sattva* is "one who is heroic, courageous and patient in contemplation of the two truths—the conventional truth and the ultimate truth." In his *Abbreviated Sutra,* Buddha himself explained that *sattva* means "one who is generous, has great wisdom, is full of energy, has entered the path of Greater Vehicle Buddhism and has put on the armor of patience and tolerance and thereby combats the defiled states of mind."

In the Tibetan text we find the phrase *thab-chig-tu zhug-pa.* This has been translated as "accompanied by" and refers to how people are seated or gathered together. *Zhug-pa* means "to sit" or "be together," while *thab-chig-tu* means "a form of discipline." Thus, the term *thab-chig-tu zhug-pa* means that the assembly was sitting together in the same disciplined state.

## THE PROFOUND APPEARANCE

*"On that occasion the Lord was absorbed in a particular concentration called the profound appearance."*

The words "on that occasion" are not simply a casual reference to the time when this teaching was given. It means an auspicious confluence of events—a point in time when everyone's positive energy ripened and they became fully prepared to receive this teaching.

"Profound" refers to profound emptiness and "appearance" here refers to the wisdom that perceives emptiness. Therefore, Buddha was involved in single-pointed concentration on the ultimate nature of reality, which was free from both coarse and subtle forms of laxity (drowsiness) and excitement (distraction). There isn't a single moment when Buddha isn't absorbed in this kind of meditative state. Lama Tsong Khapa said that this is because Buddha is constantly aware of everything that exists. In him, mindfulness is ever-present.

However, Buddha is described as doing all sorts of other things such as eating, sleeping and so on. So, what is his state during these activities? It is said that a buddha doesn't need sleep. Nor is he ever hungry or thirsty. When a buddha appears thirsty, it is just because of the nature of our own perceptions. When Buddha went begging for alms, he wasn't really in need of food but was trying to inspire bene-factors to create positive energy by giving and thus increase their own merit (*punya*). A buddha doesn't need to eat food because he already enjoys the food of concentration.

## AVALOKITESHVARA

*"Meanwhile the bodhisattva, the great being, the noble Avalokiteshvara was contemplating the profound discipline of the perfection of wisdom.*

*He came to see that the five aggregates were empty of any inherent nature of their own."*

The sutras were not necessarily spoken word by word. There are different kinds of sutras—blessed sutras, permitted sutras and spoken sutras—composed of words blessed, permitted or spoken by Buddha. These three kinds of teaching are not seen as contradictory and are all considered as teachings of Buddha. The Four Noble Truths constitute actual words spoken by Buddha himself, as do most of the teachings in the *Prajnaparamita* sutras.

The *Heart Sutra* is generally considered to be a sutra presented through Buddha's permission and so it is a permitted sutra. But within the text we find passages that seem to dwell within the two other kinds, as when Buddha says, "well said, well said" to Avalokiteshvara. It is also a blessed sutra in the sense that Buddha blessed Shariputra and gave him the confidence to ask his question.

We find innumerable bodhisattvas among the ten levels of bodhisattva realization. There are the eight close bodhisattva disciples of Buddha, for example. But of them all, it is Avalokiteshvara, Vajrapani and Manjushri who are considered to be the most important. Manjushri is the embodiment of the highest form of wisdom—that which perceives the emptiness of all phenomena. The unique quality of Vajrapani is that he is the embodiment of the enlightened power of all the buddhas.

The word "noble" used in reference to Avalokiteshvara is a translation of the Sanskrit word *arya*, which has often been translated as "superior" or "transcendental" being. Avalokiteshvara, the embodiment of the compassion of all the buddhas, always keeps his eyes open to all sentient beings in order to liberate them from suffering and the causes of suffering and to endow them with happiness and the causes of happiness. Bodhicitta is the altruistic mind of enlightenment and the bodhicitta of Avalokiteshvara is said to be cowherd-like. Just as a cowherd doesn't rest until all the cows are safe in their shelter, so too has Avalokiteshvara promised that he will not rest until he has established all sentient beings in the mind of enlightenment. He is special because he represents compassion in its most intense and ultimate form.

Avalokiteshvara's compassion is extended infinitely to all sentient beings. To him, all are equal rather than being separated into friends, adversaries and strangers. He is able to manifest simultaneously in innumerable forms. His mind is omniscient, understanding precisely and distinctly each and every aspect of phenomena and the qualities and characteristics of the paths and grounds leading to liberation and enlightenment. The text demonstrates that Avalokiteshvara understands that the five aggregates—the principal faculties that make up a sentient being—are all empty of true existence.

## SHARIPUTRA'S QUESTION

*"Through the power of the Buddha, the venerable Shariputra approached the noble Avalokiteshvara and asked him, 'How should a son of the noble lineage proceed when he wants to train in the profound discipline of the perfection of wisdom?'"*

Thus, absorbed in meditative concentration, Shakyamuni Buddha blessed and inspired his disciple Shariputra to ask Avalokiteshvara this question; that is, how should a person who wishes to follow the Mahayana path leading to enlightenment train his or her mind? "A child of the noble lineage" means someone who has the inclination of a bodhisattva or of Mahayana Buddhism. A Mahayana practitioner with keen intelligence and sharp mental faculties realizes emptiness first and then cultivates love, compassion and bodhicitta, the altruistic mind of enlightenment. One with slightly lower faculties cultivates love, compassion and bodhicitta first, and then studies and realizes emptiness.

## AVALOKITESHVARA'S ANSWER

*"The noble Avalokiteshvara replied to the venerable Shariputra, 'Whatever son or daughter of the noble lineage wants to train in the profound discipline of the perfection of wisdom should consider things in the following way. First, he or she should clearly and thoroughly comprehend that the five aggregates are empty of any inherent nature of their own....'"*

Avalokiteshvara's answer tells us that from the Buddhist point of view, men and women are equal in being able to follow spiritual practice and gain spiritual realizations. Furthermore, every phenomenon—the house in which we live, the environment, in fact everything around us—has two truths, conventional and ultimate. When we shift the focus to ourselves, we see that we also have conventional and ultimate aspects. Once we know about the emptiness of forms, we can apply the same reasoning to the other four aggregates that make up our psycho-physical personality—feeling, discriminative awareness, compositional factors and consciousness, which are also empty of true or inherent existence.

The crucial word here is "inherent." Of course the aggregates exist in a conventional sense but they do not exist in and of themselves. That is, they do not possess an objective existence. The line of philosophical reasoning is as follows. If a phenomenon were to exist in and of itself, it would not depend upon causes and conditions. If things did not depend upon causes and conditions, it would mean that results could occur without causes, which is impossible.

## THE CHARACTERISTICS OF EMPTINESS

*"Form is empty but emptiness is form. Emptiness is not other than form and form is not other than emptiness. Similarly, feelings, discernments, formative elements and consciousness are also empty. Likewise, Shariputra, are all phenomena empty. They have no defining characteristics; they are unproduced; they do not cease; they are undefiled, yet they are not separate from defilement; they do not decrease, yet they do not increase."*

In the text we find that form is emptiness and emptiness is form. In other words, form is not different from emptiness and emptiness is not different from form. In his answer to Shariputra, Avalokiteshvara says that all phenomena are empty. This does not mean that nothing exists. What it does mean is that all phenomena are empty of something. That "something" is inherent, or objective, existence. The *Heart Sutra* doesn't explicitly mention inherent or objective existence—it simply states that "form is empty"—but this is the true meaning of emptiness.

The text describes eight characteristics of emptiness, one of these being that phenomena have no defining characteristics. What this means is that phenomena have no *inherently existing* defining characteristics. So, when we contemplate this section of the *Heart Sutra,* if we conclude that nothing is produced and nothing ceases to exist, we are mistaken. The reality of phenomena is created by our perceptions and consciousness. Phenomena do exist and we cannot deny them. It is only inherent existence that does not exist. We know this because inherent existence is not apprehended to exist by any valid perception or state of mind. It is from this point of view that we speak of the self of phenomena and the self of a person as not existing.

"They are undefiled" means that even afflictive emotions and the afflictions of delusions do not inherently exist. This is precisely the reason why we can rid ourselves of them. Everybody who is not free of defilements possesses delusions, which means that all of us are defiled. But where are these defilements? Do they have form or are they formless? If they had form it would be easy to take them out and remove them, but our defilements do not have form. We can't throw them away because they are a part of our consciousness. Yet these defilements cannot contaminate the absolute nature of our mind. If they did, then when we removed them we would also be removing our mind. Then, when we reached enlightenment, we would be without consciousness altogether.

Therefore, we must understand that our defilements and our consciousness are not inseparable. When our clothes get dirty, the dirt is not the same as the cloth. When we wash our clothes it is the dirt that comes out. Our clothes remain intact. So remember, when we get rid of defilements we are not getting rid of our mind. When we engage in the activities of accumulating positive energy and wisdom, thus purifying our defilements, what we are really doing is purifying defilements *on* the mind rather than *in* the mind.

In the line "yet they are not separate from defilement," we see how even the liberated side of phenomena, the freedom from defilements, does not inherently exist. Where it says "they do not decrease," we see that we have to work to develop qualities to decrease defilements or negativities. They do not diminish in and of themselves.

The eight characteristics of emptiness presented here describe the "three doors to liberation." The first one presents emptiness as the door to liberation. The next five characteristics represent what we call "signlessness" (*tsen-ma me-pa*) as the door to liberation. The last two characteristics represent "aspirationlessness" (*mön-pa me-pa*) as the door to liberation.

THE FIVE BODHISATTVA PATHS

In Mahayana Buddhism, we present five progressive levels, or paths, of spiritual realization by which an aspiring bodhisattva travels towards enlightenment—the paths of accumulation, preparation, seeing (insight), meditation and no more learning.

On the first two paths, those with bodhisattva inclinations are primarily engaged in listening to and contemplating the teachings on emptiness. As they progress along the paths of seeing and meditation, they begin cultivating the awareness of emptiness that arises through meditation. The obscurations to liberation and the obscurations to omniscience are the two main types of mental affliction that obstruct one's attainment of buddhahood and each of the five paths acts as an antidote to these obscurations.

*The path of accumulation.* Within the path of accumulation we find three levels—the great, the intermediate and the initial, or small. At first, practitioners simply listen to the teachings. They do contemplate to some degree, but mainly they just listen. On the great, or advanced, level of the path of accumulation, it is possible for certain practitioners to actually ascertain or realize emptiness, at least conceptually. It is on this path that one gains the two collections of merit (virtuous actions) and wisdom. Although one has not yet gained any real clarity in relation to emptiness, one is clearly accumulating the necessary causes for that clarity.

*The path of preparation.* There are four levels on this path—heat, peak, patience and supreme mundane qualities, or supreme Dharma.

On these levels, practitioners comprehend emptiness conceptually. At the heat level, the meditator attains a clear conceptual awareness of emptiness within a meditative stabilization. The peak level marks a point at which the virtuous roots that have been cultivated previously will no longer decrease or be lost. At the patience level the meditator develops familiarity with the concept of emptiness and overcomes fear of it. When practitioners have reached this level and beyond, they are safe from falling into the three bad migrations, the unfortunate states of rebirth. At this stage, based upon their own valid reasoning, their conceptual understanding of emptiness is so powerful that they gain a deep understanding of the infallibility of the law of karmic actions and result. Even though they may have already-accumulated negativities, they cease to create fresh ones. At the level of supreme mundane qualities, the cognizing subject no longer appears while one is in meditative equipoise. Subject and object do appear, but the meditator no longer consciously perceives them. The path of preparation is also called the connecting path, as it connects us to the path of seeing.

*The path of seeing.* As one progresses on the four levels of the path of preparation, one moves onto the path of seeing. It is while the meditator is on this path that he or she directly experiences emptiness for the first time. Here, one does not create any new karmic actions to cause rebirth in samsara. There is a quote—"seeing the truth, there is no precipitation"—which means that when one sees the ultimate truth of emptiness, just as a person with good eyesight will not walk off a cliff, one does not create any new karmic action that will precipitate one to be reborn into cyclic existence. The path of seeing is the first of the ten spiritual grounds of the bodhisattva, the remaining nine of which lie within the path of meditation.

*The path of meditation.* On the path of meditation, when practitioners are in the state of meditative equipoise on emptiness, they experience it directly, with no duality whatsoever.

*The path of no more learning.* This means that we literally have no more to learn. We have reached the state of perfection. We have reached enlightenment.

## The object of negation

The first thing with which we have to deal in our meditation on emptiness is identification of what is called in Buddhism "the object of negation" or "the object of refutation." The object of negation is the concept of the inherent existence of phenomena and the subsequent grasping at the existence of phenomena. As we find in the great bodhisattva Shantideva's *Guide to a Bodhisattva's Way of Life*, "Without coming into contact with the inherent thing, one cannot comprehend the absence of that thing." This means that without precisely identifying and recognizing the concept that you are refuting (the object of negation), you are not going to understand emptiness. After all, emptiness is established by way of refuting something. That something is inherent existence.

The main purpose of meditating on emptiness is to be able to counteract grasping at inherent existence. This grasping is the other object of negation. If we don't understand what is being refuted, then even if we try to meditate on emptiness, our meditation will not counteract our grasping. We will be shooting an arrow without knowing where the target is.

When we talk about the object of negation we are speaking of two kinds—one that exists and one that does not. To be able to identify the two types of object of negation, we have to check our perception and the habitual way we perceive things. For example, how do we perceive the self to exist? We perceive it to exist in and of itself. This idea of the inherent existence of the self is what we call a "non-existent object of negation"; our grasping at self is an "existent object of negation." We perceive and then we grasp. We use two different methods to deal with these two types of object of negation. We use authentic scriptural quotations to deal with the object of negation that does exist and valid reasoning to deal with the one that does not.

Thus, we should try to imagine how we individually perceive the self to exist and where we perceive it as existing. Once we recognize the fallibility of the idea of a self, it is easy to recognize how we grasp at other phenomena. But in order to be able to understand the non-existence of the self, we first have to know what we mean by the term "inherent existence." What are the criteria by which we judge whether something exists inherently? First, it should exist independently; second, it should not rely upon causes and conditions. Does the self exist this way? Upon analysis we can see that it does not. The self exists dependently. It is dependent upon the collection of our five physical and mental aggregates. This is the first level of how to meditate on emptiness.

EMPTINESS OF THE AGGREGATES

*"This being the case, Shariputra, in terms of emptiness there exist no forms, no feelings, no discernments, no formative elements, no consciousness..."*

Remember that Avalokiteshvara is explaining how to train the mind in the perfection of wisdom. The key point is that while we are on the path of meditation, what exists for us in the state of meditative equipoise on emptiness is just emptiness and nothing else. Conventional phenomena do not exist for that kind of wisdom. We do not even perceive the basis upon which emptiness is established. We perceive emptiness directly, nakedly and non-conceptually.

When one first begins to meditate on emptiness, one also perceives the conventional phenomena that are the basis upon which emptiness is established. Eventually, our perceptions become like "water poured into water"—undifferentiable from one another. We no longer experience any duality existing between our perceptions and they become of "one taste." This is why we say that all conventional phenomena have been exhausted for aryas in the state of meditative equipoise on emptiness.

What Avalokiteshvara means when he says "in terms of emptiness there exist no forms" is that conventional forms do not exist in this state. It is common for people to fall into the extreme of nihilism and misinterpret this as meaning that forms do not exist at all. This is as mistaken a view as the extreme of absolutism, or eternalism. If a person is not receptive or "ripened" they can easily misconstrue the meaning of emptiness.

There is a story of a *mahasiddha*, a great Indian master, who took shelter from the midday heat in the carcass of an elephant. The elephant's insides had been eaten by worms and its body was empty like a cave. The mahasiddha meditated here and gained direct experience into emptiness. One day, the local king invited the mahasiddha to his palace and asked him to teach about emptiness. The mahasiddha entered a deep meditative state and started pointing at things saying, "That doesn't exist, this doesn't exist, they don't exist." He wasn't denying the existence of phenomena; what he meant was that nothing exists inherently, in and of itself. But his audience completely misunderstood him. The king became very angry and sentenced the mahasiddha to death.

Some time later, the king invited another great master to his palace. This master first spoke about basic things, such as the practice of refuge and the law of karma and its results. Eventually, he began to guide the king and his attendants into an understanding of emptiness. Because of his great merit, the king was able to gain direct insight into emptiness through these teachings. But when he entered into meditative equipoise on emptiness, he couldn't help repeating the first mahasiddha's statements, "That doesn't exist, this doesn't exist, they don't exist." It was then that he understood how truly realized the first mahasiddha had been. (Now, you might ask, if the mahasiddha was so realized why did he have to die in such a miserable way? This has something to do with the infallible law of karmic action and result. When unwanted problems come to us we must understand that this is the result of our own negative karmic actions, but we should not conclude that the practice of Dharma doesn't work.)

Just as forms do not exist for an arya's wisdom in meditative stabilization on emptiness, so the remaining aggregates—feelings, discriminative awareness, compositional factors and consciousness do not exist for such wisdom. When we read this statement we must understand that we are not denying the conventional existence of the five aggregates but just their inherent existence. We can see that the aggregates exist dependently, arising as they do from certain causes and conditions.

## OBJECTS, FACULTIES AND PERCEPTIONS

*"...no eyes, no ears, no noses, no tongues, no bodies, no minds; no visual forms, no sounds, no smells, no tastes, no tactile sensations, no mental objects. There exist no visual elements, no mental elements, and no elements of mental consciousness."*

As you recite the *Heart Sutra* and come across these lines, you must understand that what is being stated here is that none of these things exist for the wisdom of an arya in a state of meditative equipoise on emptiness—especially on the path of meditation. In the *Heart Sutra*, we find eighteen elements of phenomena. There are six objects, six faculties and six perceptions, all of which are empty of true existence. Emptiness pervades all phenomena. For example, when we are directly perceiving the emptiness of the true existence of eyes, we are only perceiving the basis upon which the eyes exist, but not the eyes themselves.

Visual forms, sounds, smells, tastes, tactile sensations and mental objects are the six objects, or objective conditions, of the six faculties. The six faculties are eyes, ears, nose, tongue, body and mind. Visible form is an object of eye consciousness, sound is an object of ear consciousness, smell is an object of nose consciousness, taste is an object of tongue consciousness, touch is an object of tactile consciousness and thought is an object of mental consciousness. The six faculties are the basis for the arising of a particular consciousness. For example, the eyes are the basis for the consciousness that perceives visual forms.

Sometimes we speak of the twelve sources. These refer to the six objects and the six faculties combined. The twelve sources give rise to the six perceptions of seeing, hearing, tasting, smelling, touching, and thinking. "Source" is the English translation of the Tibetan word *kye-che*, meaning "that which gives rise to" and "door through which things are perceived," as well.

THE TWELVE LINKS OF DEPENDENT ARISING

*"There exist no ignorance and no exhaustion of ignorance, no aging and death and no exhaustion of aging and death."*

This sentence refers to the chain of twelve dependent links, or the chain of dependent origination. This describes the process by which we are continually falling into cyclic existence. This chain or sequence of events begins with 1) ignorance and follows with 2) karmic formation, 3) consciousness, 4) name and form, 5) sensory fields, 6) contact, 7) feelings, 8) attachment, 9) grasping, 10) becoming, or existence, 11) birth and 12) aging and death.

Buddha has pointed out the need for us to understand and meditate on the twelve dependent links in both sequential and reverse order. In sequential order we are seeing the afflictive side of phenomena—that which pulls us into cyclic existence, or samsara. In reverse order we see the unafflictive side of phenomena—that which liberates us from cyclic existence. Contemplating the twelve links in sequential order, we gain insight into the limitations of cyclic existence; contemplating them in reverse order, we learn how to liberate ourselves from cyclic existence.

1) *Ignorance.* The first link is ignorance (*ma-rig-pa*). Ignorance is the root cause of cyclic existence. It misperceives the self of a person and the reality of all phenomena and causes us to grasp at ego and material things. But the wisdom that perceives selflessness sees the emptiness of the self and all other phenomena. Ignorance and selflessness contradict each other. It is very important to individually focus on our own ignorant grasping at self and to know that this root delusion gives rise to all others.

All problems stem from this root—the ignorant grasping at self, or I. This is the real troublemaker in our lives. To be able to fight the tendency to grasp at a self we have to prepare our minds through study and practice of the three higher trainings—training in higher ethics, higher concentration and higher wisdom.

Training in higher ethics lays a firm, solid foundation on which to build our other practices. Monks and nuns have their own ethics to keep, but even people who haven't taken any vows should refrain from engaging in negative actions, particularly the ten negative actions.

Having laid a foundation of ethics, one can then practice in the higher training of concentration. Just as a woodcarver needs strong arms to cut wood, we need to develop the strong arm of concentration through mindfulness and introspection. Without mindfulness and introspection, our meditation will be very weak and ineffectual.

Once we have cultivated concentration, we need to cultivate wisdom, particularly the wisdom perceiving emptiness. This is our superior weapon; with it we can cut through the grasping at self. It is our woodcutter's ax, with which we can chop through our dense forest of ignorance. All of our spiritual activities, no matter what they may be, should be geared towards destroying our habitual grasping at self and cultivating the wisdom perceiving emptiness so that we can experience ultimate reality.

In the pictorial representation of the wheel of life, ignorance is depicted as a blind man, walking without any guide. Such a person is always uncomfortable and confused wherever he or she goes. Ignorance prompts us to create karmic actions that then become the cause of all our problems and suffering. Just as a blind person moving towards a precipice is certain to fall, whatever actions spring from ignorance are bound to bring about problematic results. Buddha made the statement, "Because this exists, that arises." In the same way, because ignorance exists, karmic formation naturally follows.

2) *Karmic formation.* The second link is karmic formation (*du-che kyi là*). Karmic actions arise out of ignorance and are capable of precipitating our rebirth into samsara. There are two kinds of ignorance, that pertaining to the infallibility of the law of karmic actions and result and that pertaining to the ultimate reality of phenomena. Ignorance of the law of karma motivates us to do negative, or nonmeritorious, actions. These actions ripen in cyclic existence, especially in the three unfortunate states of rebirth—the hell, hungry ghost and animal realms.

Ignorance related to misunderstanding the ultimate nature of reality can make us do karmically positive or neutral actions. Positive actions stemming from this type of ignorance can ripen within fortunate states of rebirth—in the human, demigod or deva realms. In the drawing of the wheel of life, this link is depicted as a potter rotating his wheel. It is karma that spins and molds us in cyclic existence.

3) *Consciousness.* The third link is consciousness (*nam-she*). There are two kinds of consciousness—causal and resultant. Causal consciousness exists with the performance of a karmic action. As that action—good or bad—comes to an end, it leaves an imprint on our consciousness. The consciousness that receives that imprint is the causal consciousness.

Resultant consciousness is activated by an imprint, or latency, that was deposited earlier on. The consciousness that enters the womb of a mother is an example of this. It is the consciousness that arises as a result of certain karmic actions in the past.

Say, for example, that out of ignorance we kill someone and don't purify that action. The action leaves an imprint on our consciousness, which thus becomes a causal consciousness. Some day this imprint will precipitate an unfortunate rebirth; the consciousness that goes towards that conception is the resultant consciousness.

In the wheel of life, consciousness is shown as a monkey. When a monkey inside a house with windows on all four sides looks out each window it sees different views, but it is still the same monkey. Similarly, it is our single consciousness upon which imprints of our karmic actions are deposited and then activated at different times to bring about certain results. This is how we are born into various states in cyclic existence.

4) *Name and form.* The fourth link is called "name and form" (*ming-zug*). Those born from the womb (as opposed to those born through miraculous power) possess the five aggregates that constitute the psycho-physical personality. The first aggregate is "form." The remaining four—feelings, discriminative awareness, compositional factors and consciousness—are called "name" because they do not

have the concrete quality of form. Form is considered to begin when the consciousness enters the womb and absorbs into the mixture of sperm and egg. In the wheel of life, the dependent link of name and form is depicted as a boat. Just as we need a boat to cross a river, in order to cross over into a physical being in cyclic existence we depend on name and form.

5) *Sensory fields.* The fifth link is called "origination" or "sources" (*kye-che*). As I mentioned before, there are twelve sense fields altogether—one for each of the six senses and one for each of the objects of the six senses, including mind. There are eye and visual forms seen, ear and sounds heard and so forth. In the wheel of life, this dependent link is represented by a fortress because our senses encompass and concretize our experience of the world.

6) *Contact.* The sixth link is called "contact" or "touch" (*reg-pa*). It refers to the interaction of an object, a sense faculty and a consciousness. Before this contact, although our faculties are fully developed, we cannot perceive anything or distinguish one thing from another. Only when there is a union of these three things can perception or discriminative awareness occur. When there is a meeting of attractive object, sense faculty and consciousness, a pleasant feeling arises. Similarly, when there is a contact of unattractive object, sense faculty and consciousness, an unpleasant feeling is experienced. In the wheel of life, contact is depicted iconographically by a man and woman in sexual union.

7) *Feelings.* Contact naturally gives rise to the seventh link of feeling (*tsor-wa*). We talk about three types of feelings—pleasant, unpleasant and neutral—all of which arise from some kind of contact. When we see something, there follows a sense of attraction or aversion and a value judgment about what we are seeing, which stimulates these feelings further. In the wheel of life, feelings are represented by a man with an arrow stuck in his eye. This describes our sensitivity and how, when feelings arise, we notice them immediately.

8) *Attachment.* Feelings precipitate the eighth link, attachment, craving or desire (*se-pa*). When we experience a pleasant feeling, we desire to not be separated from it. When we feel trapped in a problem, we experience the desire to be free from it. In our everyday life we experience all sorts of feelings. It is possible to have feelings without attachment, but the feelings we are talking about here are the kind that stem from ignorance. If we eliminate ignorance, we will experience feelings without attachment. Not surprisingly, attachment is depicted in the wheel of life as a person indulging in intoxicating liquor. In some treatises, attachment is likened to someone scratching an itchy skin irritation—it feels pleasant at first, but it is actually creating the conditions for more and more itching.

9) *Grasping.* Attachment gives rise to the ninth link, grasping (*len-pa*), which is an intensified form of attachment. There are four kinds of grasping—grasping at sense objects (forms, sounds, smells, tastes and tactile objects); grasping at wrong, or distorted, views; grasping at improper ethics and disciplines, seeing them as worthy; and grasping at the inherent existence of the five aggregates. In the wheel of life this dependent link is depicted as a person picking fruit.

10) *Becoming, or existence.* Grasping gives rise to the tenth link, becoming, or existence (*si-pa*). A karmic action leaves an imprint on our mental consciousness. At the time of death, that imprint is activated by craving and grasping. In this way, the karma becomes fully prepared to precipitate the next rebirth and a being about to be reborn feels a powerful attraction towards its future parents, who are about to engage in sexual union.

11) *Birth.* The eleventh link is rebirth (*kye-wa*). It occurs from this fully ripened karmic action. In Buddhism, rebirth is considered to have taken place when the consciousness enters the womb of the mother at conception and later culminates in the act of physical birth.

12) *Aging and death.* The final link is aging and death (*ga-shi*). Aging

begins from the moment of conception. Death is technically defined as the complete exhaustion of the aggregates, when the life energy, or life force, comes to an end. The dependent link of birth necessarily gives rise to aging and death, and if one dies under the power of karmic actions and delusions one is necessarily born under their influence. Yet, if someone born from delusions and contaminated karmic actions becomes an arhat and attains liberation, such a person does not die under the influence of delusion, and his or her rebirth is not influenced by them.

*Summary.* Ignorance is the cause of all karmic formation, which gives rise to consciousness. Consciousness allows for name and form and the sensory fields, which prepare the way for contact. Contact elicits feelings that stimulate attachment and create grasping. Grasping is the condition that brings about existence, which in turn precipitates rebirth and leads to aging and death. The twelve dependent links can be brought under four headings:

- *Precipitating causes*—ignorance, karmic formation and causal consciousness. These are the links that instigate our rebirth into cyclic existence. Ignorance is like a farmer, karmic formation is the seed sowed by the formation of ignorance and causal consciousness is likened to a field.
- *Accomplishing causes*—craving, grasping and becoming. Just as water, manure and sunlight prepare the seed for growth, in the same way, craving, grasping and becoming activate the karmic action and prepare it to bring about its result.
- *Precipitated results*—resultant consciousness, name and form, sources, contact and feelings are brought about by the accomplishing causes.
- *Accomplished result*—aging and death.

When we study the twelve dependent links in reverse order we are really trying to reverse the entire process. We are trying to put an end to aging and death by preventing birth and trying to put an end to ignorance, which stops the whole cycle from repeating. What uproots ignorance is the wisdom realizing emptiness, and when ignorance is eliminated, karmic formation does not arise. The whole purpose of studying and meditating on emptiness is to break this chain of twelve dependent links.

## THE EMPTINESS OF SUFFERING

*"In the same way there exist no suffering, no origin of suffering, no cessation, no path, no wisdom, no attainment and no lack of attainment."*

Neither suffering, the path, attainment nor the lack of these things truly exist for an arya's wisdom in the state of meditative equipoise on emptiness. Even the wisdom that realizes the Four Noble Truths does not exist for this wisdom. We must not misinterpret "no attainment" to mean that we cannot attain buddhahood or the qualities of a buddha. We can. It simply means that this attainment does not exist for an arya who is in a state of meditative stabilization because in this state he or she sees only emptiness and not conventional phenomena. There also exists no lack of attainment, so neither does failure appear for this kind of wisdom.

## THE NATURE OF BODHISATTVAS

*"Therefore, Shariputra, since bodhisattvas have no attainment, they depend upon and dwell in the perfection of wisdom; their minds are unobstructed and unafraid. They transcend all error and finally reach the end point: nirvana."*

This passage deals with the path of meditation in general and the meditative stabilization of a bodhisattva on the final stage of the tenth ground in particular. This vajra-like state of meditation becomes an antidote to the last obstacle to enlightenment. What is meant by "they depend upon and dwell in the perfection of wisdom" is that bodhisattvas are completely free from any fabrications when absorbed in the nature of emptiness, being completely engaged in that state.

When we talk about purifying negativity, we find two kinds of defilement—coarse, or gross, and subtle. Just as the coarse dirt on our clothes is easier to wash away, coarse defilements are easier to get rid of. Subtle stains penetrate our clothes more deeply and are harder to clean away; the final obscurations to omniscience, even though the smallest in magnitude, are the toughest to eradicate. We need the most powerful weapon to destroy them. This weapon is the vajra-like meditative state.

"Their minds are unobstructed and unafraid" tells us that such bodhisattvas, having trained their mind in stages, from the path of accumulation all the way up to the final stage of the tenth bodhisattva ground, have abandoned many of the obscurations along the way, including fear.

Then comes the phrase, "They transcend all error." We talk about four kinds of error, sometimes called the "four distortions"—perceiving that which is impure as pure; perceiving that which is painful as pleasurable; perceiving impermanent phenomena as permanent; and perceiving that which is selfless as having self. Bodhisattvas are free from these errors and also from the error of the two extremes—solitary peace and cyclic existence.

When we emerge from the vajra-like meditative state, we achieve the liberated path and attain the final enlightenment of buddhahood. This state is described by the Sanskrit word *nirvana*, which means, "beyond distress" or "beyond sorrow." These are the sorrow and distress of the solitary peace of personal liberation and the sorrow and distress of cyclic existence. Nirvana refers not just to personal liberation but to complete enlightenment as well.

Buddha's great compassion prevents him from falling into the extreme of solitary peace. If he did, he wouldn't be able to work continuously for the benefit of other beings. Like the bodhisattvas, he also has the fully developed perfection of wisdom and is thus free from cyclic existence. Foe destroyers, arhats of the Lesser Vehicle, who have liberated just themselves from samsara, are still trapped in solitary peace and, unlike bodhisattvas, cannot work for the welfare of other sentient beings.

THE UNIVERSAL PATH

*"All the buddhas of the past, present and future have depended, do and will depend upon the perfection of wisdom. Thereby they became, are becoming and will become unsurpassably, perfectly and completely awakened buddhas."*

From this we understand that the perfection of wisdom is the universal path trod by all the buddhas of the past, present and future. The perfection of wisdom is also referred to as the Great Mother because it gives birth to the buddhas of the three times. In both Buddha's sutras and tantras we find skillful means, or method (*upaya*), referred to as father-like and wisdom (*jnana*) as mother-like. This wisdom gives birth, metaphorically speaking, to the three different states of liberation—those of the hearers, solitary realizers and bodhisattvas.

THE MANTRA OF THE PERFECTION OF WISDOM

*"Therefore, the mantra of the perfection of wisdom is a mantra of great knowledge; it is an unsurpassable mantra; it is a mantra that is comparable to the incomparable; it is a mantra that totally pacifies all suffering. It will not deceive you, therefore know it to be true!"*

In both sutra and tantra, the word mantra has the same connotation—protecting the mind. Practitioners who practice mantra are protecting their minds from fears and danger. The perfection of wisdom fulfills the same purpose. It is called a mantra here because when we cultivate the wisdom gone beyond, this practice also works to protect us from fear and danger.

The perfection of wisdom is "a mantra of great knowledge" in the sense that of all the various kinds of wisdom, it is the greatest—the real antidote to ignorance. The mode of apprehension of ignorance is incompatible with the mode of apprehension of the wisdom of emptiness, which directly contradicts the grasping at self. It is "unsurpassable" inasmuch as we cannot find any other wisdom that has such power to free us from both suffering and its causes. The perfection of wisdom leads us to the non-abiding state of enlightenment, and because of this it "is comparable to the incomparable."

Another interpretation of this passage can be related to the five paths. "Therefore the mantra of the perfection of wisdom" relates to the path of accumulation; "Is a mantra of great knowledge" relates to the path of preparation; "It is an unsurpassable mantra" relates to the path of seeing; "It is a mantra that is comparable to the incomparable" relates to the path of meditation; and "It is a mantra that totally pacifies all suffering" relates to the path of no more learning, or enlightenment. The five paths of the Greater Vehicle are differentiated from one another from the point of view of wisdom, or insight, not from the point of view of method, or skillful means. The way in which everything actually exists—the ultimate nature of phenomena—is the way that it is perceived by the perfection of wisdom. It is this perception that can take us to the state of enlightenment.

As we train our minds in the perfection of wisdom, we should do so together with the practices of the other five perfections, or the skillful means of method. We should not isolate wisdom from method or method from wisdom. If we do not practice the two together, we will never achieve enlightenment. The integration of method and wisdom is essential.

The importance of this was expressed well by the first Dalai Lama in his praise to Lama Tsong Khapa when he said, "Integrating method and wisdom together, you have actualized the three enlightened bodies. Most glorious spiritual master, please bless me." By practicing method and wisdom on the five paths, we can abandon all obstacles and finally reach the state of non-abiding enlightenment.

THE MEANING OF THE MANTRA

*"I proclaim the mantra of the perfection of wisdom, TAYATHA GATE GATE PARAGATE PARASAMGATE BODHI SVAHA. Shariputra, it is in this way that the great bodhisattvas train themselves in the profound perfection of wisdom."*

The *Heart Sutra* can be condensed from a Mantrayana or tantric

Buddhist point of view into the one-line mantra, TAYATHA GATE GATE PARAGATE PARASAMGATE BODHI SVAHA.

The word TAYATHA means, "it is like this." GATE means "go" as an exhortation. So GATE GATE means "go, go," meaning that we should go onto the path of accumulation and then go further onto the path of preparation. PARAGATE literally means "go beyond" and PARASAM-GATE means "go thoroughly beyond." It is telling us to go beyond the paths of accumulation and preparation and onto the paths of seeing and meditation towards supreme enlightenment.

The first GATE or "go" is for beginners with Mahayana inclinations, those practitioners who haven't yet entered the Mahayana path but who are cultivating compassion and the perfection of wisdom. It means go to the path of accumulation of the Greater Vehicle. When practitioners spontaneously and naturally experience bodhicitta, they have already entered the Mahayana path of accumulation.

The second GATE also means "go." When practitioners have gone to the path of accumulation they should go on to the next path, which is the path of preparation. It is on this path that practitioners can conceptually understand emptiness. Practitioners who have traversed the paths of hearers or solitary realizers may have already realized emptiness directly when they enter the path of Mahayana.

When we have reached the path of preparation we should go beyond to the path of seeing. When we reach the path of seeing we are already on the first spiritual ground of bodhisattvas. We are then told to "go thoroughly beyond." We should not get stuck on the path of seeing but go higher up onto the path of meditation. BODHI is enlightenment and SVAHA means to become stabilized in the state of enlightenment. So the meaning of the entire mantra is, "It is this way: Go, go, go beyond, go thoroughly beyond, go to enlightenment and become stabilized there."

CONCLUSION

*"At that moment the Lord arose from his concentration and said to the noble Avalokiteshvara, 'Well said, well said. That is just how it is, my*

*son, just how it is. The profound perfection of wisdom should be practiced exactly as you have explained it. Then the tathagatas will be truly delighted.' When the Lord had spoken these words, the venerable Shariputra and the bodhisattva, the great being, the noble Avalokiteshvara, and the entire gathering of gods, humans, asuras and gandharvas were overjoyed, and they praised what the Lord had said."*

When Avalokiteshvara and Shariputra finish their dialogue, Buddha rises from his meditative state. He authenticates the words of Avalokiteshvara and congratulates him on his presentation of the perfection of wisdom. His explanation delights not only Buddha himself but all the enlightened beings of the ten directions and the buddhas of the three times. After the teaching, everybody in the gathering committed themselves to following the perfection of wisdom, while others who were not yet ready made fervent prayers that they would soon be able to do so.

# THREE

# GREAT COMPASSION

The life stories of Buddha and other enlightened teachers shouldn't be regarded as just interesting tales but should be seen as practices for us to follow and paths by which we can grow spiritually. Buddha stated that compassion is the core of his teachings. This compassion should be all-pervasive and non-discriminatory. We should minimize harmful actions towards others and try to increase the scope of our compassion to bring more and more people and sentient beings into its fold. We also need to cultivate the determined wish to be liberated and develop a true aspiration for enlightenment.

It is not so hard to aspire to be liberated from the problems of cyclic existence, but we need also to have the same wish in reference to samsara's prosperity and happiness. Pain in cyclic existence does not last but neither does pleasure, so we should not cling to samsara's temporary marvels. To be true Dharma practitioners, we must consider our future lives to be more important than the present one. We should consider others to be more important than ourselves and spiritual activity to be more important than worldly activity. Of course, all these things will come to us gradually. We need to train our mind in stages before we can experience this kind of change in attitude.

Remember that all good things happen to us through the kindness of others. It is only in relation to other sentient beings that we can do our practice. If sentient beings didn't exist, we couldn't practice at all or create the positive energy and positive actions through which we receive peace and happiness. Thinking in this way, we can see the kindness of all sentient beings.

As Dharma practitioners, our practice involves two things—

purifying our negativities and accumulating positive energy and wisdom. You can do these things in relation to the Three Jewels, sentient beings or both. Therefore, experienced lineage masters who have deep spiritual understanding tell us that sentient beings are as kind to us as Buddha himself. This might seem inconceivable at first, but in terms of the inspiration for our practice there is little difference between them. Normally, although we may accept certain sentient beings as being kind to us, we also become selective. We exclude those who have been bad to us and include only those whom we consider worthy. But if we exclude some beings, then logically all others should be excluded as well. We must create a sense of equanimity, a balanced attitude, in relation to all sentient beings—friends, adversaries and strangers.

If we really want to work for the benefit of others, it is essential to cultivate great compassion. For those who wish to pursue the path of the bodhisattva in Mahayana Buddhism, it is as important to cultivate great compassion and altruism as it is to cultivate the perfection of wisdom. It is not very difficult to generate compassion for ourselves, but it is a great deal harder to cultivate the same compassion for others. Yet this should be our goal, however hard it may be.

FOUR

# DEDICATION

Let us dedicate our positive energy to the flourishing of Buddhadharma throughout the world.

Let us dedicate our positive energy to the long life of His Holiness the Dalai Lama. May his sacred mandalas of body, speech and mind be unharmed by negative intentions and actions. May he and other great masters be successful in fulfilling their dreams and visions for benefiting all sentient beings.

Let us dedicate our positive energy to all spiritual communities throughout the world, so that they may flourish in their study, contemplation and meditation.

Let us dedicate our positive energy to the elimination of the problems in our world, such as famine and war. May everyone in this and other world systems experience peace, happiness and harmony.

Let us dedicate our positive energy to ourselves and to other Dharma practitioners, so that we may overcome all obstacles to spiritual development.

Let us dedicate our positive energy to ourselves and to all sentient beings, so that we can purify the obscurations to liberation and omniscience and quickly reach enlightenment.

# GLOSSARY

*(Skt = Sanskrit; Tib = Tibetan)*

*aggregates (Skt: skandha).* The psycho-physical constituents that make up a sentient being: form, feeling, discriminative awareness, compositional factors and consciousness.

*Ajatashatru (Skt).* Early Indian king who imprisoned and killed his father, Bimbisara. Realizing the enormity of this sin and guided by Buddha, he purified this negativity and became an arhat.

*arhat (Skt).* Literally, foe destroyer. A person who has destroyed his or her inner enemy, the delusions, and attained liberation from cyclic existence.

*arya (Skt).* Literally, noble. One who has realized the wisdom of emptiness.

*Avalokiteshvara (Skt; Tib: Chenrezig).* The buddha of compassion. A male meditational deity embodying fully enlightened compassion.

*bodhicitta (Skt).* The altruistic determination to reach enlightenment for the sole purpose of enlightening all sentient beings.

*bodhisattva (Skt).* Someone whose spiritual practice is directed towards the achievement of enlightenment. One who possesses the compassionate motivation of bodhicitta.

*buddha (Skt).* A fully enlightened being. One who has removed all obscurations veiling the mind and has developed all good qualities to perfection. The first of the Three Jewels of Refuge. See also *enlightenment.*

*Buddhadharma (Skt).* The teachings of the Buddha. See also *Dharma.*

*buddha nature.* The clear light nature of mind possessed by all sentient beings; the potential for all sentient beings to become enlightened by removing the two obscurations, the obscurations to liberation (see also *delusion*) and the obscurations to omniscience.

*Buddhist (Tib: nang-pa).* One who has taken refuge in the Three Jewels of Refuge: Buddha, Dharma and Sangha and who accepts the philosophical world view of the "four seals": that all conditioned things are impermanent, all contaminated things are dissatisfactory in nature, all phenomena are empty and nirvana is true peace.

*Chandrakirti* (*Skt*). The sixth century AD Indian Buddhist philosopher who wrote commentaries on Nagarjuna's philosophy. His best known work is *A Supplement to the Middle Way* (*Madhyamakavatara*).

*compassion* (*Skt: karuna*). The wish for all sentient beings to be separated from their mental and physical suffering. A prerequisite for the development of bodhicitta. Compassion is symbolized by the meditational deity Avalokiteshvara.

*consciousness.* See *mind.*

*cyclic existence* (*Skt: samsara; Tib: khor-wa*). The six realms of conditioned existence, three lower—hell, hungry ghost (Skt: *preta*) and animal—and three upper—human, demigod (Skt: *asura*) and god (Skt: *sura*). It is the beginningless, recurring cycle of death and rebirth under the control of delusion and karma and fraught with suffering. It also refers to the contaminated aggregates of a sentient being.

*delusion* (*Skt: klesha; Tib: nyön-mong*). An obscuration covering the essentially pure nature of mind, being thereby responsible for suffering and dissatisfaction; the main delusion is ignorance, out of which grow desirous attachment, hatred, jealousy and all the other delusions.

*Dharma* (*Skt*). Spiritual teachings, particularly those of Shakyamuni Buddha. Literally, that which holds one back from suffering. The second of the Three Jewels of Refuge.

*dharmakaya* (*Skt*). The "truth body." The omniscient mind of a fully enlightened being, which, free of all coverings, remains meditatively absorbed in the direct perception of emptiness while simultaneously cognizing all phenomena. The result of the complete and perfect accumulation of wisdom. One of the three holy bodies of a buddha. See also *rupakaya.*

*dualistic view.* The ignorant view characteristic of the unenlightened mind in which all things are falsely conceived to have concrete self-existence. To such a view, the appearance of an object is mixed with the false image of its being independent or self-existent, thereby leading to further dualistic views concerning subject and object, self and other, this and that and so forth.

*emptiness* (*Skt: shunyata*). The absence of all false ideas about how things exist; specifically, the lack of the apparent independent, self-existence of phenomena. Sometimes translated as "voidness."

*enlightenment* (*Skt: bodhi*). Full awakening; buddhahood. The ultimate goal of Buddhist practice, attained when all limitations have been removed from the mind and one's positive potential has been completely and perfectly realized. It is a state characterized by infinite compassion, wisdom and skill.

*equanimity.* Absence of the usual discrimination of sentient beings into friend, enemy and stranger, deriving from the realization that all sentient beings are equal in wanting happiness and not wanting suffering and that since beginningless time, all beings have been all things to each other. An impartial mind that serves as the basis for the development of great love, great compassion and bodhicitta.

*five paths.* The paths along which beings progress to liberation and enlightenment; the paths of accumulation, preparation (conjunction), seeing (insight), meditation and no more learning.

*form body.* See *rupakaya.*

*Gelug* (*Tib*). The Virtuous Order. The order of Tibetan Buddhism founded by Lama Tsong Khapa and his disciples in the early fifteenth century.

*Great Vehicle.* See *Mahayana.*

*hearer* (*Skt: shravaka*). One branch of the Hinayana. Practitioners who strive for nirvana on the basis of listening to teachings from a teacher. Cf. *solitary realizer.*

*Hinayana* (*Skt*). Literally, Small, or Lesser, Vehicle. It is one of the two general divisions of Buddhism. Hinayana practitioners' motivation for following the Dharma path is principally their intense wish for personal liberation from conditioned existence, or samsara. Two types of Hinayana practitioner are identified: hearers and solitary realizers. Cf. *Mahayana.*

*ignorance* (*Skt: avidya; Tib: ma-rig-pa*). Literally, "not seeing" that which exists, or the way in which things exist. There are basically two kinds, ignorance of karma and ignorance of ultimate truth. The fundamental delusion from which all others spring. The first of the twelve links of dependent arising.

*inherent existence.* What phenomena are empty of; the object of negation, or refutation. To ignorance, phenomena appear to exist independently, in and of themselves, to exist inherently. Cf. *emptiness.*

*Kagyu (Tib)*. The order of Tibetan Buddhism founded in the eleventh century by Marpa, Milarepa, Gampopa and their followers.

*karma (Skt; Tib: lä)*. Action; the working of cause and effect, whereby positive actions produce happiness and negative actions produce suffering.

*lama (Tib; Skt: guru)*. A spiritual guide or teacher. One who shows a disciple the path to liberation and enlightenment. Literally, heavy—heavy with knowledge of Dharma.

*lam-rim (Tib)*. The graduated path. A presentation of Shakyamuni Buddha's teachings in a form suitable for the step-by-step training of a disciple. The lam-rim was first formulated by the great India teacher Atisha (Dipankara Shrijnana, 982–1055) when he came to Tibet in 1042. See also *three principal paths*.

*Lesser Vehicle*. See *Hinayana*.

*liberation (Skt: nirvana; Tib: thar-pa)*. The state of complete liberation from samsara; the goal of a practitioner seeking his or her own freedom from suffering (see also *Hinayana*). "Lower nirvana" is used to refer to this state of self-liberation, while "higher nirvana" refers to the supreme attainment of the full enlightenment of buddhahood.

*lo-jong*. See *mind training*.

*Madhyamaka (Skt)*. The middle way; a system of analysis founded by Nagarjuna based on the *Prajnaparamita* sutras of Shakyamuni Buddha and considered to be the supreme presentation of the wisdom of emptiness. This view holds that all phenomena are dependent arisings and thereby avoids the mistaken extremes of self-existence and non-existence, or eternalism and nihilism. It has two divisions, Svatantrika and Prasangika.

*Mahayana (Skt)*. Literally, Great Vehicle. It is one of the two general divisions of Buddhism. Mahayana practitioners' motivation for following the Dharma path is principally their intense wish for all mother sentient beings to be liberated from conditioned existence, or samsara, and to attain the full enlightenment of buddhahood. The Mahayana has two divisions, Paramitayana (Sutrayana) and Vajrayana (Tantrayana, Mantrayana). Cf. *Hinayana*.

*mantra (Skt)*. Literally, mind protection. Mantras are Sanskrit syllables usually recited in conjunction with the practice of a particular meditational deity that embody the qualities of that deity.

*merit.* Positive imprints left on the mind by virtuous, or Dharma, actions. The principal cause of happiness. Accumulation of merit, when coupled with the accumulation of wisdom, eventually results in rupakaya.

*mind* (*Skt: citta; Tib: sem*). Synonymous with consciousness (*Skt: vijnana; Tib: nam-she*) and sentience (*Skt: manas; Tib: yi*). Defined as that which is "clear and knowing"; a formless entity that has the ability to perceive objects. Mind is divided into six primary consciousnesses and fifty-one mental factors.

*mind training* (*Tib: lo-jong*). A genre of teaching that explains how to transform the mind from self-cherishing to cherishing others, eventually leading to the development of bodhicitta.

*Nagarjuna* (*Skt*). The second century AD Indian Buddhist philosopher who propounded the Madhyamaka philosophy of emptiness.

*nihilist.* In the context of this book, someone who, upon hearing about emptiness, comes to the mistaken conclusion that nothing exists; for example, that there's no cause and effect of actions or no past and future lives.

*nirvana* (*Skt*). See *liberation.*

*Nyingma* (*Tib*). The "ancient" order of Tibetan Buddhism, which traces its teachings back to the time of Padma Sambhava, the eighth century Indian tantric master invited to Tibet by King Trisong Detsen to clear away hindrances to the establishment of Buddhism in Tibet.

*Object of negation, or refutation* (*Tib: gag-cha*). What is conceived by an awareness conceiving true existence; the appearance of inherent existence.

*paramita* (*Skt*). See *six perfections.*

*Paramitayana* (*Skt*). The Perfection Vehicle; the first of the two Mahayana paths. This is the gradual path to enlightenment traversed by bodhisattvas practicing the six perfections through the ten bodhisattva levels (*Skt: bhumi*) over countless eons of rebirth in samsara for the benefit of all sentient beings. Also called the Sutrayana. See also *Vajrayana.*

*Prajnaparamita* (*Skt*). The perfection of wisdom.

*pratyekabuddha* (*Skt*). See *solitary realizer.*

*purification.* The eradication from the mind of negative imprints left by past non-virtuous actions, which would otherwise ripen into suffering. The most effective methods of purification employ the four opponent powers of reliance, regret, resolution and the application of antidotes.

*refuge.* The door to the Dharma path. A Buddhist takes refuge in the Three Jewels, fearing the sufferings of samsara and having faith that Buddha, Dharma and Sangha have the power to lead him or her out of suffering to happiness, liberation or enlightenment.

*rupakaya (Skt).* The "form body." The holy body of a fully enlightened being, it is the result of the complete and perfect accumulation of merit. It has two aspects. The *sambhogakaya,* or "enjoyment body," is the form in which the enlightened mind appears to benefit highly realized bodhi-sattvas; the *nirmanakaya,* or "emanation body," is the form in which the enlightened mind appears to benefit ordinary beings. See also *dharmakaya.*

*samsara (Skt).* See *cyclic existence.*

*Sangha (Skt).* Spiritual community; the third of the Three Jewels of Refuge. Absolute Sangha are those who have directly realized emptiness; relative Sangha are ordained monks and nuns.

*sentient being (Tib: sem-chen).* Any unenlightened being; any being whose mind is not completely free from gross and subtle ignorance.

*Shakyamuni Buddha* (563–483 BC). Fourth of the one thousand founding buddhas of this present world age. Born a prince of the Shakya clan in north India, he taught the sutra and tantra paths to liberation and enlightenment; founder of what came to be known as Buddhism. (From the *Skt: buddha*—"fully awake.")

*shravaka (Skt).* See *hearer.*

*six perfections (Skt: paramita).* Generosity, ethics, patience, enthusiastic perseverance, concentration and wisdom. See also *Paramitayana.*

*solitary realizer (Skt: pratyekabuddha).* One branch of the Hinayana. Practitioners who strive for nirvana in solitude, without relying on a teacher. Cf. *hearer.*

*sutra (Skt).* A discourse of Shakyamuni Buddha; the pre-tantric division of Buddhist teachings stressing the cultivation of bodhicitta and the practice of the six perfections. See also *Paramitayana.*

*Sutrayana (Skt).* See *Paramitayana.*

*tantra (Skt; Tib: gyüd ).* Literally, thread, or continuity; the texts of the secret mantra teachings of Buddhism. Often used to refer to these teachings themselves. See also *Vajrayana.* Cf. *sutra.*

*Tantrayana (Skt)*. See *Vajrayana*.

*Theravada (Skt)*. One of the eighteen schools into which the Hinayana split not long after Shakyamuni Buddha's death; the dominant Hinayana school today, prevalent in Thailand, Sri Lanka and Burma, and well represented in the West.

*thought transformation*. See *mind training*.

*Three Baskets (Skt: tripitaka)*. The three divisions of the Dharma: vinaya, sutra and abhidharma.

*Three Jewels (Tib: kon-chog-sum)*. The object of refuge for a Buddhist: Buddha, Dharma and Sangha.

*three principal paths*. The three main divisions of the lam-rim: renunciation, bodhicitta and right view.

*Tripitaka (Skt)*. See *Three Baskets*.

*Triple Gem*. See *Three Jewels*.

*truth body*. See *dharmakaya*.

*Tsong Khapa, Lama Je* (1357–1417). Founder of the Gelug tradition of Tibetan Buddhism and revitalizer of many sutra and tantra lineages and the monastic tradition in Tibet.

*twelve links of dependent arising*. The twelve steps in the evolution of cyclic existence: ignorance, karmic formation, consciousness, name and form, sensory fields, contact, feelings, attachment, grasping, becoming, or existence, birth, and aging and death.

*true existence*. See *inherent existence*.

*Vajrayana (Skt)*. The adamantine vehicle; the second of the two Mahayana paths. It is also called Tantrayana or Mantrayana. This is the quickest vehicle of Buddhism as it allows certain practitioners to attain enlightenment within one lifetime. See also *tantra*.

*wisdom*. Different levels of insight into the nature of reality. There are, for example, the three wisdoms of hearing, contemplation and meditation. Ultimately, there is the wisdom realizing emptiness, which frees beings from cyclic existence and eventually brings them to enlightenment. The complete and perfect accumulation of wisdom results in dharmakaya. Cf. *merit*.

# SUGGESTED FURTHER READING

(The brief comment after each title indicates its relevance to this book, *Mirror of Wisdom*.)

Gyatso, Tenzin, the Fourteenth Dalai Lama. *The Meaning of Life*. Tr. Jeffrey Hopkins. Boston: Wisdom Publications, 1992. (Teachings on the twelve links of dependent arising.)

————. *Opening the Eye of New Awareness*. Tr. Donald S. Lopez, Jr. Boston: Wisdom, revised edition, 1999. (Teachings on the three higher trainings; explanations of many technical terms, for example, the five aggregates.)

————. *Transcendent Wisdom*. Tr. B. Alan Wallace. Ithaca: Snow Lion Publications, 1994. (Commentary on the wisdom chapter of Shantideva's *Bodhicaryavatara*.)

Hopkins, Jeffrey. *Meditation on Emptiness*. Boston: Wisdom, 1983. (Classic work on Mahayana philosophy, especially Prasangika-Madhayamaka.)

————. *Emptiness Yoga*. Ithaca: Snow Lion, second edition, 1995. (Follow-up work; philosophy made practical.)

Rabten, Geshe. *Echoes of Voidness*. Tr. Stephen Batchelor. Boston: Wisdom, 1983. (Commentaries on the wisdom chapter of Chandrakirti's *Madhyamakavatara* and the *Heart Sutra*.)

Rinchen, Geshe Sonam. *Atisha's Lamp for the Path to Enlightenment*. Tr. Ruth Sonam. Ithaca: Snow Lion, 1997. (Commentary on the original lam-rim text.)

————. *The Six Perfections*. Tr. Ruth Sonam. Ithaca: Snow Lion, 1998. (Explanation of the essential bodhisattva practices.)

Shantideva. *A Guide to the Bodhisattva's Way of Life*. Tr. Stephen Batchelor. Dharamsala: Library of Tibetan Works and Archives, 1979. (The quintessential text of Mahayana Buddhism.)

Sopa, Geshe Lhundup & Jeffrey Hopkins. *Cutting Through Appearances*. Ithaca: Snow Lion, 1989. (Detailed explanation of the four schools of Buddhist philosophy.)

# THUBTEN DHARGYE LING

THUBTEN DHARGYE LING ("Land of Flourishing Dharma") is a center for the study and practice of Tibetan Buddhism. It was founded in 1978 by Geshe Tsultim Gyeltsen, who gives regular teachings on Buddhist texts and classes in meditation.

Over the years, Geshe Gyeltsen has invited many eminent masters to teach at his center, including Kyabje Song Rinpoche and Lati Rinpoche. Thubten Dhargye Ling has also sponsored four visits to Los Angeles by His Holiness the Dalai Lama.

In 1984, His Holiness taught Lama Tsong Khapa's *The Three Principal Aspects of the Path* and gave an Avalokiteshvara initiation. In 1989 His Holiness taught Togme Zangpo's *Thirty-seven Practices of a Bodhisattva* and conferred the Kalachakra initiation. In 1997, he gave a commentary on Nagarjuna's *Precious Garland* and a Shakyamuni Buddha initiation. This book has been published in honor of His Holiness's June, 2000, visit, when he will teach Atisha's *Lamp for the Path to Enlightenment* and Lama Tsong Khapa's *Lines of Experience.*

Thubten Dhargye Ling
3500 East 4th Street
Long Beach, CA 90804, USA
(562) 621-9865
www.tdling.com

REBECCA MCCLEN NOVICK is a writer and documentary filmmaker. She is the co-producer of "Strange Spirit," an award-winning film about human rights in Tibet and is the author of *Fundamentals of Tibetan Buddhism.*

LINDA GATTER is an editor for the LAMA YESHE WISDOM ARCHIVE and the Maitreya Project. A former director of Land of Medicine Buddha, an FPMT center in California, she has studied Tibetan Buddhism since meeting the Dharma in 1978.

NICHOLAS RIBUSH is director of the LAMA YESHE WISDOM ARCHIVE. A former Australian physician and a student of Tibetan Buddhism since 1972, he co-founded Wisdom Publications with Lama Yeshe in 1975. Over the years, he has edited and published many teachings by His Holiness the Dalai Lama, Lama Yeshe, Lama Zopa Rinpoche and other Tibetan lamas.

# Lama Yeshe Wisdom Archive

The LAMA YESHE WISDOM ARCHIVE is delighted and honored to be working with Venerable Geshe Tsultim Gyeltsen and Thubten Dhargye Ling on the auspicious occasion of His Holiness the Dalai Lama's June, 2000, visit to Los Angeles.

The ARCHIVE was established by Lama Thubten Zopa Rinpoche in 1996 to manage the collected works of Lama Thubten Yeshe and Lama Zopa Rinpoche. At present it contains about 6,000 cassette tapes of the Lamas' teachings going back to the early 1970s, when they began teaching Dharma to Westerners at Kopan Monastery, Kathmandu, Nepal.

The work of the ARCHIVE falls into two categories, archiving and dissemination. The archiving part includes collection and preservation of recorded material, transcription of untranscribed tapes and management of transcripts. Dissemination mainly entails editing of checked transcripts for publication and distribution of edited material. We prepare manuscripts for publication as books for the trade, articles for various magazines and booklets for free distribution.

Several free booklets are currently available, including Lama Yeshe's *Becoming Your Own Therapist* and *Make Your Mind an Ocean* and Lama Zopa Rinpoche's *Virtue and Reality*, *A Chat About Heruka* and *A Chat About Yamantaka* (the latter two for initiates only). We have also recently published Lama Zopa Rinpoche's *Teachings from the Vajrasattva Retreat*, a 700-page volume for sale.

You will also find many teachings on our Web site, www.lamayeshe.com. The ARCHIVE is a section of the Foundation for the Preservation of the Mahayana Tradition (FPMT).

For copies of our free booklets or more information, please contact

LAMA YESHE WISDOM ARCHIVE
PO Box 356
Weston, MA 02493, USA
Tel. (781) 899-9587
Email nribush@cs.com or wendycook@compuserve.com

# What to do with Dharma teachings

The Buddhadharma is the true source of happiness for all sentient beings. Books like the one in your hand show you how to put the teachings into practice and integrate them into your life, whereby you get the happiness you seek. Therefore, anything containing Dharma teachings or the names of your teachers is more precious than other material objects and should be treated with respect. To avoid creating the karma of not meeting the Dharma again in future lives, please do not put books (or other holy objects) on the floor or underneath other stuff, step over or sit upon them, or use them for mundane purposes such as propping up wobbly tables. They should be kept in a clean, high place, separate from worldly writings, and wrapped in cloth when being carried around. These are but a few considerations.

Should you need to get rid of Dharma materials, they should not be thrown in the rubbish but burned in a special way. Briefly: do not incinerate such materials with other trash, but alone, and as they burn, recite the mantra OM AH HUM. As the smoke rises, visualize that it pervades all of space, carrying the essence of the Dharma to all sentient beings in the six samsaric realms, purifying their minds, alleviating their suffering, and bringing them all happiness, up to and including enlightenment. Some people might find this practice a bit unusual, but it is given according to tradition. Thank you very much.

# Dedication

Through the merit created by preparing, reading, thinking about and sharing this book with others, may all teachers of the Dharma live long and healthy lives, may the Dharma spread throughout the infinite reaches of space, and may all sentient beings quickly attain enlightenment.

In whichever realm, country, area or place this book may be, may there be no war, drought, famine, disease, injury, disharmony or unhappiness, may there be only great prosperity, may everything needed be easily obtained, and may all be guided by only perfectly qualified Dharma teachers, enjoy the happiness of Dharma, have love and compassion for all sentient beings, and only benefit and never harm each other.

GESHE TSULTIM GYELTSEN was born in the Kham province of eastern Tibet in 1923. Inspired by his uncle, who was a monk, he entered the monastery at the age of seven, where he studied sutra and tantra under Geshe Jampa Thaye, a highly respected teacher from Sera Monastery. At sixteen he entered Ganden Monastery to study for his geshe degree. He joined Ganden's Shartse College, where the renowned abbot, Song Rinpoche, took a special interest in his progress.

At the time of the 1959 Tibetan uprising against China's oppression, he escaped from Tibet and resettled in Dalhousie, in northern India, where he continued his studies. On passing his exams with honors, he was awarded the highest degree, that of *lharampa* geshe.

In 1963, he went to Sussex, England, where he taught Tibetan refugee children at the Pestalozzi International Children's Village. He moved to the United States in 1976 and for a short time taught meditation and Tibetan language at the University of California's campuses at Santa Barbara and Los Angeles. When Geshe-la's students asked him to start a Buddhist center, he founded Thubten Dhargye Ling, now located in Long Beach, California. Here, he teaches meditation and classes on various Buddhist subjects, holds retreats and celebrates religious holidays with his students. He has also founded centers in Alaska, Texas, Colorado, Mexico and England and travels extensively to teach at these and other Buddhist centers. He is the author of *Compassion: The Key to Great Awakening, a Commentary on the "Eight Verses of Mind Training" and the "Thirty-seven Practices of a Bodhisattva."*

Geshe-la is known for his great compassion and personal warmth, yet he retains a very traditional and uncompromising approach to teaching the Dharma. His strength of vision and devotion to his practice transcend time and culture, and he continues to inspire his students with the legacy he has brought from Tibet.

LOTSAWA TENZIN DORJEE is a prominent native translator of Tibetan Buddhist subjects. He received his formal education at the Institute of Buddhist Dialectics in Dharamsala, India, and at California State University at Long Beach, where he was awarded his BA in Communication Studies.

Beginning in 1981, he worked for more than a decade at the Library of Tibetan Works and Archives (LTWA) in the Department of Philosophy and Language Studies. As a senior staff member of LTWA's Research and Translation Bureau, he translated for His Holiness the Dalai Lama and many other eminent masters. In 1991 he was translator for Lati Rinpoche's tour of North America.

He has translated a number of important books, including *Generous Wisdom* and the recently re-released, *Nagarjuna's Seventy Stanzas, A Buddhist Psychology of Emptiness.*

In 1993, he joined Thubten Dhargye Ling, where he has translated for Geshe Tsultim Gyeltsen as well as benefiting the center in innumerable other ways.